JURY RIGGING IN THE COURT OF PUBLIC OPINION

An Analysis of
Swift Justice: Murder and Vengeance in a California Town
by Harry Farrell, and the
Brooke L. Hart Kidnapping,
Murder, and Lynching Case
in San Jose, California in 1933.

JOHN D. MURPHY

Jury Rigging in the Court of Public Opinion

Published by Lulu

For information and to order copies please go to WWW.JURYRIGGINGINTHECOURTOFPUBLICOPINION.COM

ISBN # 978-1-4303-2607-6

To Paula

Table of Contents

Introduction 1

Part I Overview 3

Political Bullwhips 4
Swift Justice 5

Part II Kidnapping, Murder, and Manhunt 13

The Kidnapping 16
Sole Eyewitness Accounts 19
The Wallet in San Francisco Bay 20
The Interminable Week-End 21
Lost in the Shuffle 23
Assessment of the Culprits 24
First Ransom Note 24
Second Ransom Note 25
Second and Third Ransom Calls 27
Third Ransom Letter 29
Fourth Ransom Call 31

Part III The Confessions 33

Analysis 33
Thurmond's Confession 36
Holmes's Confession 43
Contradictions in the Confessions 48
Public Reaction 50
Principal Discrepancies 53
Abandoned Studebaker 53
Verification of the Eyewitness Accounts 53
Brooke Hart's Wallet 59

Jack Holmes's Alibi Chain 60
Alibi One 60
Alibi Two 60
Alibi Three 61
Alibi Four 61
Alibi Five 61
Corroborating Evidence 64
Other Discrepancies: 66
Thurmond Identifies Brooke Hart 66
Holmes Wipes Off Fingerprints 66
Holmes Hits Hart on Head 66
Murder Method 67
Kidnapping Plan 67
Gun Purchase 67
Unqualified Mastermind 67
Thurmond Climbs under the Bridge 68
Ransom Meetings 68
The Wallet Toss 69
Thurmond's Failed Ransom Call 69
"Some Woman" 69
Sacramento Postmark 70
Thurmond Gets Second Ransom Note 70
Holmes outside Garage 70

Part IV Mastermind and Foil 71

The Kidnapping Plan 76
Mastermind 77
Holmes's Motivation 82
Holmes's Means 85
Thurmond's Motivation 86
Thurmond's Means 87
Criminal Propensities 88

Part V The Lynching 91

Part VI FBI Handwriting Analysis 110

Part VII Thurmond and Holmes 112

Part VIII Veracity of Confessions 116

Part IX Middle-Class Mob 118

Part X Conclusion 121

Exhibits 125

One: Executive Summary
Two: The 'Real' Kidnappers
Three: Kidnapping, Murder, and Lynching Chronology

End Notes 150

Selected Bibliography 151

Acknowledgments 151

John D. Murphy 152

Introduction

Convicted in the court of public opinion, four days before Thanksgiving in 1933, two men accused of the kidnapping and murder of Brooke L. Hart were lynched in a park in San Jose, California. It is the only time in United States history in which both the jury and the executioners included members of law enforcement, elected and public officials, business and civic leaders, the press, thousands of middle-class citizens, and the governor of a state.

A mob estimated by newspapers to be between 5,000 to 15,000 men, women, and children witnessed the two men being forcibly taken from the county jail and lynched. Both the day before and day after, then California Governor James "Sunny Jim" Rolph had promised to pardon anyone convicted of the lynching, so despite thousands of witnesses, scores of reporters, and hundreds of news photographs, no one was ever held responsible—including the governor.

The next morning, and continuing for nearly sixty years until former *San Jose Mercury* reporter, columnist, and editor, Harry Farrell, wrote the seminal insider account of the event, *Swift Justice: Murder and Vengeance in a California Town,* thousands of these lynching participants observed an eerily serendipitous conspiracy of silence.

Swift Justice honors the conventional version of history that in November 1933 both caused and justified the lynching. This version marginalizes objective analysis, and the weighting of facts that materially challenge the belief that the two men were guilty.

Jury Rigging in the Court of Public Opinion unfolds the Brooke L. Hart kidnapping and murder investigation, and analyzes how the case against the two accused men was engineered and politicized. It also documents how evidence was manipulated, and a criminal pathology imagined three generations later in *Swift Justice* to justify why two local men—one married with two children and the other who had suffered a severe head injury as a child—confessed to a high-profile kidnapping and murder and literally had their lives taken from them at the hands of their fellow citizens.

The facts relied upon to assert the guilt of the two men in *Swift Justice* also materially evidence their innocence. When these are linked to information from other sources and an objective analysis undertaken, it establishes conclusively that Thomas Harold Thurmond and Jack Holmes did not kidnap and murder Brooke L. Hart.

Part I Overview

The lynching of Harold Thurmond and Jack Holmes for the kidnap and murder of Brooke Hart, in San Jose, California in November 1933 was a singular event in American history. Never before or since has contempt for the rule of law been so collectively and overtly manifested by law enforcement (including the FBI), public officials, community leaders, everyday citizens, and the press.

This blistering scorn permitted an estimated 5,000 to 15,000 men, women, and children to jam a city park, cheer an assault on the county jail across the street, witness, and then literally celebrate two lynchings. The exploitation of honest public feeling, and the surly contempt for the rule of law that gave rise to these lynchings, endure to this day perpetuated by a materially flawed depiction of the guilt of the lynch victims who were never indicted or arraigned, much less tried for the crimes of which they were accused.

Scores of newspaper reporters, photographers, and news camera operators had rushed to San Jose that Sunday night; one won a Pulitzer Prize. The next day, Northern California newspapers sold 1.2 million copies, twice the ordinary production. The *San Francisco Examiner*'s press run was 150,000 higher than usual. The *San Francisco Chronicle* issued thirteen editions carrying the EXTRA plate; sales shattered the previous mark set by the World War I armistice.[1]

Incessantly, since the discovery, that crisp fall morning, of a terribly decomposed body in the San Francisco Bay determined to be the kidnap victim, radio stations had broadcast inflammatory bulletins about the lynching.[2] A Los Angeles radio announcer featured the lynching as a "live event." A San Jose movie theater projectionist placed a slide on the screen that announced that the lynching was about to start, and the patrons surged towards the exits (p. 16).

Political Bullwhips

Asked if he would order the National Guard to stop the lynching, Governor James Rolph retorted that he would pardon the lynchers. Two hours prior to the lynching, he cancelled a trip to the western governors' conference in Boise, Idaho, to prevent his chief political rival, the lieutenant governor, from the use of the National Guard because he had left the state (p. 215).

Governor Rolph was connected both personally and politically to San Jose through former state senator, and attorney, Louis Oneal. Fellow Republican Oneal, literally Rolph's next door neighbor in the mountains on the west side of Santa Clara Valley above San Jose, was the powerful overlord of the dominant county political machine (p. 15).

During the assault on the county jail and the lynching, Oneal maintained an open phone line from his ranch to the jail

---

[1] Farrell, Harry, *Swift Justice: Murder and Vengeance in a California Town*, St. Martin's Press, 1992, P. 243.

[2] Ibid, *Swift Justice*, P. 203. NOTE: All subsequent *Swift Justice* citations are referenced in parentheses ( ).

in downtown San Jose (p. 215); with him was Raymond Cato, appointed by Rolph as the chief of the California Highway Patrol (p. 118). Three years previously, Oneal had handpicked San Jose Police Traffic Captain William J. Emig to run for Santa Clara County sheriff, and got him elected (p.15).

Oneal had joined the sheriff and FBI agents in the interrogation of suspect Thomas Harold Thurmond. Ordinarily the sheriff would have provided Thurmond's confession to the press, but it was released through Louis Oneal's law office (p. 138).

Swift Justice

Three generations after the lynchings, former *San Jose Mercury* reporter and columnist, Harry Farrell,[i] wrote the award-winning insider account of the event: *Swift Justice: Murder and Vengeance in a California Town,* St. Martin's Press, 1992. Still in the city where he was born, the locally revered Mr. Farrell passed away in 2006.

In his introduction to *Swift Justice,* Harry Farrell candidly acknowledged his bias toward the history with which he grew up:

> "I have used conventional wisdom about the case based on facts publicly aired…taking at face value the Thurmond and Holmes confessions" (p. x).

In acknowledgement of his home town prejudice, Farrell paid homage to the dramatically compelling, yet factually tenuous, tapestry of guilt woven by law enforcement, community leaders, the governor of California, the citizenry, and the press in November 1933 that created the foundation for, and was manifested by the lynchings:

> "Nowhere—neither street talk nor news reporting, nor official action—was the legal presumption of innocence even accorded lip service. The confessions of the prisoners were taken at face value; prospective efforts to repudiate them were dismissed out of hand" (p. 172).
>
> "In the court of public opinion, Jack Holmes and Thomas [Harold] Thurmond already stood convicted with no chance of appeal" (p. 158).

Farrell had tried to attain the "literal truth" (p. xi), when he wrote *Swift Justice*, but freely admitted that his representation of facts ventured well outside commonly observed journalistic standards and practices:

> "Where direct quotations are invented, their purpose was to enhance the truth (p. xi)
>
> "[W]hen sources are in conflict, obvious error, or incomplete, I have had to make educated guesses" (p. xi).
>
> "Certain matters appearing in quotation marks [sic] does not meet the same standards of exactness…in a…contemporary news story. I freely acknowledge taking liberties…to produce a narrative in human terms" (p. xi).

The acceptance of facts as "publicly aired," permitted Farrell to conform the available written record—newspaper stories, the FBI file on the kidnapping of Brooke L. Hart, and personal interviews—with the time, place, and action scenario detailed in the suspects' confessions. It also freed him from the objective analysis of facts that didn't conform to what most people believed at the time of the lynching and allowed him to conclude:

> "The preponderance of the evidence supports the long accepted version of the events" (p. x).

Both personally, and by reputation, Harry Farrell had gained unprecedented access to the key players involved in the run up to the lynching, and the lynching itself. He honored the conventional version of history because otherwise he probably would not have obtained the cooperation needed to bring even a sliver of illumination to the dark recesses of the underlying politics of the lynching. Farrell's unorthodox historical assemblage resulted in the "long accepted" version of the event largely being taken as factually accurate. The detail is accurate, but a careful analysis of salient facts will evidence that the guilt of the accused was both misperceived and misrepresented with horrific consequences.

Farrell acknowledged that he "had to deal with... inconsistencies which...cast a passing shadow" (p. x) on his account of this historical event, but spent little time in the shadow. He accorded only superficial attention to the most obvious inconsistencies in the law enforcement version of the crime and the guilt of the two suspects, and failed to critically examine the most basic, yet glaring contradictions in the confessions.

Despite its seductive and compelling narrative force, one disquieting element among stark others in *Swift Justice,* is the creation of a heretofore diabolically concealed criminal personality for Jack Holmes.

Holmes, husband and father of two young children, became, in the pages of *Swift Justice* some sixty years after his hot-blooded murder at the hands of a mob, suddenly possessed of a sinister criminal mind (p. 90). To establish this pathology, *Swift Justice* relied on factually questionable, oblique, and remote (in time), plainly superficial, idiosyncratic personal gossip that was not, and cannot be corroborated.

Swift Justice transmogrified Holmes, who was also admirably described as, "A happy man with a promising future—well liked, recognized, and respected around town" (p. 88)—into the arch-evil manipulator of his partner and foil, Thomas Harold Thurmond, " for whom submissiveness was a way of life" (p. 85):

> "Who but dim-witted eager-to-please Harold, who would happily stick his head in an oven if anyone asked him to" (p. 91).

In contrast to Jack Holmes's imagined criminal propensities, *Swift Justice*'s depiction of Thurmond was derived from family members and individuals with a lifetime familiarity with him; none of it was flattering:

> "Slow-witted" (p. ix); "backward" (p. x); "plodding" (p. 85); "queer duck" (p. 86) and, "dullard in a family of high achievers" (p. 87). "He was just not very smart; maybe he had an eight year old mentality" (p. 87).

The one constant in Thurmond's life was the "severe head injury he had suffered as a young child" (p. 87).

Another narrative conceit in *Swift Justice* is the integration of Thurmond's and Holmes's confession statements, taken independently at different points in time, into contemporaneous dialogue. The misleading effect is the verisimilitude of live interaction between the two men as they allegedly went about the cold-blooded business of the kidnap and murder of Brooke Hart. One integration places Thurmond and Holmes in a car together the day before the kidnapping:

> "[Thurmond] shall we stick around and see when he comes out again?"
>
> "Harold, the more I think about this harebrained idea, the less I like it."

> "It could be done mighty easy."
>
> "For almost three hours they waited . . . . The side door opened, and in the glow of the street lamp he [Thurmond], recognized Brooke's golden mop of hair. Holmes tentatively placed his hand on the car door handle, ready to go into action.

Then:

> "Damn!"
>
> "Alongside Brooke's trim figure had appeared the stocky frame of Alex Hart" (p. 96).

Another integration depicts the immediate aftermath of Brooke Hart's murder:

> "Seventy one new miles had been clocked on the odometer of Jack Holmes's black Chevy as he braked to a stop at Fourth and Santa Clara streets, four blocks east of where they had taken Brooke. It was now a few minutes before eight o'clock."
>
> "Jeez, Harold, I never thought I could participate in a thing like that."
>
> "I don't know how I could do it either."
>
> "Well, as long as it's done we might as well go through with it. How much should we ask?
>
> "Fifty grand."
>
> "Don't be greedy, Harold. Let's let the old man off easy. Forty thousand, OK?"
>
> "OK with me, Jack" (p. 99).

An amalgam of the confessions and the contents of the first written demand from the kidnappers was the kicker to the discussion after the murder of Brooke Hart:

> "Holmes withdrew a postcard and pencil from his pocket and, by the car's dim dome light, laboriously printed in capitals a message to Alex Hart, Sr., composing it as he went along. It was the one which began "YOUR SON IS O.K. AND TREATED WELL…." When finished, Holmes handed the card to Thurmond, who put it in his pocket along with Brooke Hart's wallet" (p. 99).

At the time this conversation had supposedly taken place, three witnesses stated Jack Holmes had been with them. The FBI analysis of ransom note handwriting released fifty years later determined that, although Thurmond and Holmes had both confessed that Holmes wrote all three ransom notes and letters, all had been written by Thurmond.

Persons unfamiliar with the factual inconsistencies in the confessions, the declarations of alibi witnesses, and the defiance of the laws of time and space that had to be manifested by Jack Holmes, readily believe the "long accepted" and emotionally compelling version of the kidnapping and murder history memorialized in *Swift Justice*.

Swift Justice is an eye-opening case study of how the highly-charged apologetics of Thurmond's and Holmes's guilt was still being exercised sixty years after their lynching.

Thurmond's partnership with Holmes in the commission of a high profile, high stakes crime, in their own cars (Thurmond had to borrow the family car), on the streets of the city in which they had spent their entire lives, is so outlandish that it served, in 1933 and serves today, as the very reason for its credibility. It is simply so unbelievable that people believe it.

Its logical ungainliness was engineered by law enforcement in 1933 (echoed in *Swift Justice)* as evidence that only two culprits as sinisterly clever as Holmes and as moronic as Thurmond could have committed a kidnap and murder in such a bewildering and appalling manner. In reality, its outlandishness is due to the case—both chronicled and imagined in *Swift Justice*—being jury rigged to convict the suspects in the court of public opinion.

Although Thurmond possessed limited mental capacity and emotional maturity, the FBI[ii] prompted members of the Hart family who had received the ransom calls to identify, by telephonic voice recognition, the dim-witted high school drop-out as the man with "a soft, unhurried, well-modulated voice" (p. 11), who made repeated ransom calls over six days.

To exercise such a pivotal role in the kidnapping, Thurmond would have had to express himself in a coherent, and for him, an unnaturally confident manner. Confronted on the ransom calls by the skeptical and highly intelligent father of the kidnap victim, Alex Hart, Thurmond would have had to think on his feet. Given the uniform characterization of Thurmond's mental acuity, it is doubtful that he had ever thought much on his feet, or in any other way.

Absent acknowledgment of its blatantly contradictory nature, *Swift Justice* relied upon the same pathologies asserted as the criminal bona fides of Holmes and Thurmond to also justify and explain why the kidnapping was, by even the most egregious examples of bone-headed criminal behavior, incoherently designed and implemented. Their "bumbling execution of the atrocity . . . verged on the comic" (p. x).

It was "comic" because the sheriff and the FBI had implanted the time, space, and circumstance of the suspects' confessions into a Procrustean bed of guilt.

Swift Justice created, as the foundation for Holmes's gross criminal ineptitude, contradictorily enough, an imaginary criminal mind:

> "To Jack Holmes, a flawless felony was something he admired . . . a botched crime was an affront. Holmes convinced himself he was smarter than those who had been caught" (p. 90).

Holmes was the criminal mastermind who, when on a bridge only eighteen miles from San Francisco where he planned to have the first ransom call made, drove over forty miles back to San Jose before he ordered Thurmond to drive some sixty miles to San Francisco, make the ransom calls, throw the wallet into the bay, and drive sixty miles back. Thurmond had to borrow his father's car to do it.

Holmes, the criminal genius, made or ordered Thurmond to make ransom calls from pay phones within one half mile of each other on consecutive nights in downtown San Jose during one of the most intensive law enforcement manhunts in California history.

Each time a ransom call was attempted, it had to go through a local operator. The Hart's phone number had to be identified, and then there was a wait to be connected. Even this wasn't sufficient to establish the kidnappers' awe-inspiring lunacy; Thurmond was arrested on a telephone 150 feet from the San Jose Police headquarters.

There was more prodigious idiocy that literally rode around; Jack Holmes used his own car with his California license plates to carry out the entire crime.

Part II Kidnapping, Murder, and Manhunt

Three quarters of a century after the lynching, San Jose neighborhoods with palatial homes and bungalows that surround the downtown retail and business district look much the same as they did in 1933, with wide, tree-lined streets, and large lots with gardens in both the front and the back. Once-ordinary architectural conceits now bring millions of dollars from people who seek the fragile purchase of period living in a congested valley of millions.

For hundreds of square miles outside the downtown neighborhood core are spread massive housing tracts, freeways, strip and shopping malls, schools and colleges. Where hundreds of thousands of fruit trees once thrived, now sprawl offices and high-tech manufacturing facilities with parking lots for tens of thousands of vehicles.

The breathtaking sight of millions of fruit blossoms that once covered much of the Santa Clara Valley each spring is not even a faint memory. What was once endearingly referred to as "Valley of Heart's Delight" is now identified by the post-industrial nickname "Silicon Valley."

San Jose in the 1930s had a population of nearly 60,000 people, yet boasted 19,000 single- family homes, and only 400 apartments (p. 26). Its remarkable middle-class wealth derived primarily from being the "largest fruit and vegetable canning center in the nation, with thirty-three canneries, and twenty-one dried fruit packing houses" (pp. 25-26). San Jose was middle-class with a vengeance that manifested itself in a manner—the lynching—still unrivaled by any other middle-class community in the United States.

> "San Joseans jealously cherished the symbols they perceived as confirmation of their culture: their twenty-one schools; their forty-six churches; the ivied tower and arcaded quadrangle of the teachers' college [then San Jose Teachers' College; today, San Jose State University], and the Spanish-tiled buildings of the nearby University of Santa Clara" (p. 27).

The beauty, safety, and relative economic security at the height of the Great Depression was something San Jose residents deeply valued and jealously guarded, and given their reaction to the kidnapping and murder of one of their own, something they defended and protected even at the cost of human life.

While today's society is greatly inured to the graphic depiction of human depravity engorged by the news and entertainment media, the citizens of an agriculturally-based community in the 1930s were stunned and horrified by, and took at face value, the descriptions of what was represented to have happened to Brooke Hart an hour and a half after he was kidnapped:

> *Taken from a car on the San Mateo Bridge in the middle of the freezing San Francisco Bay at night, Brooke Hart was bashed on the skull twice with a twenty-two pound concrete block. He was then bound hand and foot with clothesline wire, had two of the concrete blocks tied to his feet, and was tossed off the bridge into the bay. One the kidnappers climbed under the bridge to fire a volley of shots where he disappeared into the water.*

These images ignited the rage that resulted in the lynching of the two local men who had confessed to such atrocious acts.

The other volatile element stoking the anger of these otherwise decent citizens was the outsider press. At the time, San Jose was only of marginal interest to the many aggressive San Francisco newspapers, but once it was learned that the scion of a wealthy San Jose family had been kidnapped, ruthlessly competitive reporters swarmed the city. They slavered for any details, factual and mendacious, lurid and antiseptic, that would bear their by-lines and make their publishers happy through increased circulation.

Overnight, the peaceful, sleepy, bucolic, God-fearing, conservative middle-class enclave was under the microscope. Now, San Jose's informal lifestyle and insider political and business decisions that were accepted as commonplace fell under the scrutiny of a politically uncontrollable press. This unwanted attention doubtlessly contributed to San Jose's "inferiority complex," about San Francisco (p. 27).

This "inferiority complex" intensified when San Francisco was rebuilt after the 1906 earthquake. Prior to the extensive destruction of the city on the bay, the relatively pious, church-going, upstanding citizens of San Jose could be disdainful about San Francisco's "forty-six gambling joints, forty-eight whorehouses, and 537 saloons" (p. 27).

Following the earthquake, coincidentally at the hands of then Mayor James "Sunny Jim" Rolph, San Francisco became "a place of broad boulevards and handsome parks, the mercantile hub of the west, a cultural Mecca with museums, galleries, theater, opera, and symphony" (p. 27).

> "San Joseans, reacting to the splendid rebirth of the Golden Gate metropolis, were afflicted with a compulsion to disprove what they secretly feared—that

they were hopelessly, country cousins" (p. 27).

The Kidnapping

Brooke Leopold Hart was the oldest son of Alex and Nettie Hart, and the loving brother of two younger sisters, Aleese and Miriam, an "adopted" sister, Jeannette, and younger brother Alex. The children were the product of a May-December marriage between a Catholic woman and a Jewish man twenty-three years her senior. Brooke attended a Jesuit high school, Bellarmine Preparatory, and graduated the previous summer from the University of Santa Clara.

Ten weeks before he disappeared, Brooke had been feted as the "future boss," and made vice president of the family department store. L. Hart & Son employed 200 workers, and generated staggering revenues [in 1933], of $3,000,000 a year (p. 25). Brooke had received a 1933 Studebaker President convertible roadster as a graduation present, a gift whose value exceeded the yearly income of most hard-working San Jose residents.

Brooke's public persona was that of a friendly, industrious, yet carefree young man who deserved and received a great deal of respect. At the height of the Great Depression, his exotic, luxurious, and expensive car doubtlessly attracted attention and generated some jealousy. One of the duties that came with the new car was to occasionally chauffeur his father. Sixty-four-year-old Alex Hart had never learned to drive.

Just prior to 6:00 o'clock on Thursday, November 9, 1933, Brooke had left the store by an alley door that led to a parking lot at the rear of the building. Brooke had to pick up his father at the main entrance, then drive him to a meeting of the

Chamber of Commerce at the San Jose Country Club on the east side of San Jose. Afterward, Brooke was to meet his friend, Charlie O'Brien, and attend an elocution class at the DeAnza Hotel three blocks from of the department store.

After what was supposed to take five minutes turned into almost fifteen, Alex Hart had an employee check with the lot attendant. The attendant stated that Brooke had appeared a little before 6:00, chatted for a few minutes, then got into his car and headed to the exit on the Market Street side of the department store. The attendant became distracted, and looked away as Brooke, he assumed, turned the Studebaker right towards the front of the store on Santa Clara Street.

Now late, Alex Hart asked one of his employees to give him a ride to the chamber meeting. It was unlike Brooke ever to fail to perform a task, large or small.

An hour later at the Hart mansion, Brooke's youngest sister Miriam experienced car trouble as she left for a class, and had returned to the house. The telephone rang. Charlie O'Brien informed her that Brooke hadn't shown at the DeAnza Hotel (p. 7).

At the Chamber of Commerce meeting, Alex Hart was summoned to the telephone. Told by Miriam that Brooke had not met O'Brien, Alex Hart instructed Miriam to call Chief J. N. Black of the San Jose Police Department. Miriam picked up her father from the San Jose Country Club (p. 9).

Alex Hart and Miriam arrived at home around 8:00 p.m., with still no word from Brooke. Alex Hart had Miriam drive him to downtown San Jose to meet with his long-time friend, Chief John Black. Just prior to their return about 9:30 p.m., Aleese Hart, Brooke's oldest sister answered the telephone.

"Hello."

The soft voice of a male stranger inquired:

> "Is your brother missing?"
>
> "Yes, who is this?"
>
> "Is your father there?"
>
> "No, but he should be here any minute."
>
> "Your brother has been kidnapped. You'll be hearing from us" (p. 11).

Chief Black, who had already alerted the chief operator of the phone company in San Jose to trace calls to the Hart residence, contacted both the San Francisco police and Sheriff Emig who immediately put a description of Brooke's car on the state teletype. Lastly, Black woke up Special Agent in Charge Reed Vetterli of the Federal Bureau of Investigation (FBI), in his San Francisco apartment (p. 12).

At 10:30 p.m., Miriam took another call at the Hart mansion.

> "Is this Miriam?"
>
> "Yes."
>
> "Is your brother missing?"
>
> "Yes, do you know where he is?"
>
> "We have your brother. He is safe, but it will cost you $40,000 to get him back. If you ever want to see him alive again, stay away from the police. We will phone further instructions tomorrow" (p. 13).

The Hart family did not have any more contact with the kidnappers until a ransom note was received at L. Hart & Son in the afternoon mail four long days later on Monday, November 13th.

The phone trace revealed that the 9:30 call had originated from Dwyer's speakeasy at 1000 Market Street in San Francisco, and the 10:30 call from the Witcomb Hotel, also on Market Street nearer to the Embarcadero and the bay (p. 13).

Sole Eyewitness Accounts[3]

On their farm near Milpitas, seven miles east of downtown San Jose, Delphine Silveria and her daughter Isabelle, as was their custom, ate dinner at 6:00 o'clock. About 6:30, they each picked up an armload of firewood near their barn. Thirty feet away, a public road fronted their property.

Suddenly, they heard the roar of a large sedan, and a dark, long-hooded sedan, stopped near their barn, and the headlights were turned off. Three men were in it. A few minutes later a convertible with a canvas top and a man on each running board, stopped next to the larger car. A man got off the running board, walked over to the larger car.

> "Well, we got him all right."

The light-haired driver of the convertible was marched to the sedan.

> "Get in big boy."
>
> "Are you sure we're on the right road?" one of the men asked.

---

[3] FBI Brooke L. Hart Kidnapping File

> "Yes," another replied. "Keep straight ahead, and then turn down into Milpitas and on to Oakland Road. Head for Stockton, and shoot to Sacramento."

One of the men got into the convertible, and then both cars sped away. The mother and daughter had no telephone to report what they had witnessed. The following Monday after she had visited relatives and learned of the kidnapping, Delphine Silveria contacted Sheriff Emig.

Near midnight at the San Jose Country Club, the manager closed up, and then drove home to Milpitas. As he approached his home on Evans Road, he noticed the faint headlight beams of a parked car. He stopped to check it. It was empty, with nothing apparently amiss but the faint headlights. His wife informed him it had been there since 7:00 o'clock. The sheriff later confirmed by the license plate that it was Brooke Hart's Studebaker (p. 14). It was the same convertible seen by Delphine and Isabelle Silveria.

The Wallet in San Francisco Bay

Friday, the day after Brooke's disappearance, a deck hand on a fuel tanker spotted a wallet on a previously submerged guardrail. The tanker had fueled the luxury liner, *Lurline,* at Pier 32 in San Francisco. The California driver's license, library card, gasoline credit cards, and business cards were all in the name of Brooke L. Hart.

Swift Justice noted that the "Tanker tied up at 5 p.m. . . . and . . . around midnight began pumping oil. At some point the tanker rose in the water, and its guardrail broke the surface" (p. 46). It can be approximated that the guardrail didn't rise above the waterline until mid-early morning.

The San Francisco police examined the wallet and found that it was "damp, not soaked through. The ink on some of the ID cards were smeared, not pulpy. " Based on the condition of the wallet, "Officers concluded that the wallet had not been under the water for any length of time" (p. 47).

The fact that the wallet was damp, not soaked, evidenced that it had landed onto the guardrail when it was above the waterline.

The Interminable Week-end

The Hart family encountered deadly silence from the kidnappers after the bizarrely personal ransom call that Miriam Hart took on Thursday night and the Friday discovery of Brooke's wallet. The family and law enforcement personnel could not imagine just who in the hell held Brooke Hart's life in their hands.

While lurid stories about the kidnapping—accurate, wildly speculative, and downright fabrications—sold tens of thousands of additional newspapers, the sheriff's department and the FBI tracked fruitless lead after fruitless lead.

The owner of a speakeasy recalled Brooke with a woman around 9:30 the night of the kidnapping. A woman stated that she saw Brooke's car in downtown San Jose shortly after 7:00 p.m. (the Studebaker President she saw belonged to the manager of San Jose's J.C. Penny store).

Saturday following the Friday morning discovery of the wallet, FBI agents flew to Los Angeles to determine whether Brooke Hart or anyone in contact with him had been passengers or stowaways on the *Lurline* that had arrived from San Francisco.

No one was allowed to leave the ship until it had been searched and the identity of each passenger and crew member verified. Among the passengers who took the ship to attend the Stanford-versus-University of Southern California football game in Los Angeles, was Babe Ruth. No evidence appeared that Brooke Hart, any acquaintance, or the kidnappers had been ever on the ship, much less tossed his wallet onto the guardrail of the fuel tanker.

The examination of Brooke's Studebaker turned up no fingerprints.

An L. Hart & Son employee reported, however, that he had seen "A dark 1931 Buick sedan carrying two well-dressed men parked in Lightstone Alley [next to L. Hart & Son], at 5:45 p.m. for the last ten days" (p. 48). It had not been seen since the kidnapping.

The employee's description of the size, make, and color of the sedan matched the description of the car seen by Delphine and Isabelle Silveria near their barn one half hour after Brooke Hart left the L. Hart & Son parking lot.

The investigators also became aware of a suspicious incident involving Brooke some three weeks previously:

> "As Brooke had been parking his car not far from the store, two hard-looking men in another machine had cut in on him, attempting to pin him to the curb. With his engine still running, he had quickly shot away, out of the trap" (p. 33).

Brooke had only informed his father the day before he disappeared.

Lost in the Shuffle

The desperate confusion over the kidnapper's failure to call with ransom delivery instructions only increased with the sightings of Brooke that ranged from Orland 100 miles north of San Jose, to Los Angeles 400 miles to the south. During this time, a small paragraph appeared in the *San Francisco Chronicle*:

> "Police last night were investigating a report that a young man answering Hart's description, accompanied by two men, had crossed the San Mateo Bridge Thursday night in a closed sedan" (p. 40).

Unknown to the newspapers, but reported to the Hayward, California police, two men who had gathered driftwood near the eastern shore south of the San Mateo Bridge on the night of the kidnapping not only saw, but heard something:

> "About 7:25 they had watched an automobile drive onto the darkened span, stop somewhere out over the water, and after a time, turn back. As the car had stopped, a man's voice had cried, 'Help, help!' and 'Leave me alone!' Finally, they had heard, 'I can't hold on much longer'" (p. 51).

The men had made their way along the shore toward the sound of the voice, but found no one. The next morning, Hayward police had gone out on the mud flats on the eastern shore of the San Mateo Bridge, but didn't find anything suspicious (p. 51).

Assessment of the Culprits

San Jose Police Chief Black believed that the kidnappers were intimately familiar with San Jose, its environs, and the Hart family:

> "This is local talent. The kidnappers obviously knew too much about Brooke's habits, his family, and his friends to be an outsider. The ransom caller used Miriam's name as only a friend or acquaintance would. And only someone familiar with the lay of the land around San Jose would have picked remote Evans Road as the spot to abandon Brooke's car" (p. 39).

First Ransom Note

As he went through L. Hart & Son's November 13th Monday mail, a manager spotted a small envelope with a Friday midnight postmark (the day following the kidnapping), from Sacramento, California. He observed FBI instructions on how to handle a possible ransom note (p. 55), and used tweezers to place the envelope into a cellophane sheath.

At the Hart mansion, the envelope was opened and a postcard removed:

> *"YOUR SON IS O.K. AND WILL BE TREATED WELL. ONE MORE PEEP TO THE POLICE WILL BE HIS FINISH. YOU HAVE MADE -1- SQUAWK ANOTHER WILL BE TOO BAD. WE WILL HAVE $40,000 YOU CAN GET 500-20'S (UNMARKED) 2000-10'S—200-$5'S PUT IT IN A SATCHEL (BLACK) BE READY TO TAKE A WEEKS [sic] TRIP ON AN HOUR NOTICE. GET INTO THE STUDE*

> *RDSTR HAVE RADIO INSTALLED. WHEN TOLD TO GO YOU WILL TAKE ORDERS FROM K.P.O. [NBC radio station], YOU BETTER DO AS TOLD."* [4]

The advisement that ransom instructions would be broadcast on a radio that had to be installed in Brooke's conspicuous Studebaker (which had a radio) was absurdly ridiculous. The contents of the ransom note:

> "Reinforced the growing conviction that the kidnappers were bumbling novices. It betrayed a lack of preparation, and sloppy execution, and was devoid of criminal craftiness" (p. 56).

FBI Special Agent in Charge Reed Vetterli "Studied the postcard and decided it was the work of a crank. Its crudity offended him" (p. 56).

The most monumental blunder by the kidnappers was that they had tossed Brooke's wallet into the San Francisco Bay:

> "The discovery of Blake's wallet…signaled the abductors' amateurism. They had surrendered what would have been their best credential of authenticity in ransom negotiations" (p. 56).

Second Ransom Note

Alex Hart had no contact with any of the kidnappers following the receipt of the first written ransom demand until the next day. A letter postmarked in San Francisco at 6:30 p.m. on Monday, November 13th, was contained in Tuesday November 14th's L. Hart & Son mail:

---

[4] FBI File

"WE PRESUME YOU HAVE GOTTEN OUR LETTER FROM SACRAMENTO. YOU HAVE MONEY AS DEMANDED. INDICATE SAME WITH NUMERAL IN THE MARKET STREET WINDOW OF YOUR STORE LIKE THIS: (1). YOU WILL BE ADVISED WHEN TO START YOUR TRIP AS NOTED IN FORMER NOTE. AS LONG AS THE CONTENTS OF THESE NOTES ARE KNOWN TO YOU ALONE BROOKE IS SAFE. BY NOW YOU KNOW FEDERALS OR ANYONE ELSE IS POWERLESS TO BRING BROOKE TO YOU EXECEPT THROUGH US.

"WHEN A.J. HART, WHO WILL CARRY THE MONEY, STARTS HIS TRIP HE WILL CARRY MONEY IN BLACK SATCHEL (SMALL) BESIDE HIM IN SEAT OF STUDE, ROADSTER, IF ANYONE FOLLOWS THE CAR OR KNOWS ITS ERRAND BROOKE WILL NOT BE RETURNED ALIVE. OUR NEXT CONTACT WILL TELL YOU WHERE TO GO AND BE PREPARED TO START ON THE MINUTE. YOUR EVERY MOVE IS BEING OBSERVED— AWAIT FURTHER CONTACT."[5]

The demand that Alex Hart personally deliver the ransom in Brooke's Studebaker evidenced that the kidnapper's knowledge of the Hart family was rudely superficial. During his entire life in San Jose, the exceedingly well-known Alex Hart had never driven an automobile. For the residents of San Jose, most of whom were probably lifetime patrons of L. Hart & Son, such knowledge would be common.

---

[5] FBI File

Second and Third Ransom Calls

On Tuesday night, the 14th of November, Brooke Hart's friend, Charlie O'Brien, entered the sidewalk from the garage where he parked his car when:

> "A thin-faced stranger approached from the passenger side, and reached for the door handle as if to climb in. Apparently reconsidering, the man turned and sped away on foot. O'Brien only got a fleeting look at the blank, humorless face.... The fellow had jug handle ears" (p. 63).

When O'Brien arrived home, the telephone rang "the caller...was so casual that O'Brien took him for some friend" (p. 63).

> "Hello, is this Charlie?"
>
> "Yes."
>
> "I have a message for Mr. Hart. Get this: Tell him to place the money beside him on the seat of Brooke's car, right away. And head to L.A. Before he gets there he'll be relieved of the money by a man in a white mask" (p. 63).

O'Brien hurried to the Hart residence to inform the family and FBI agents. Alex Hart answered a telephone when it rang about 8:45 p.m. It marked the first time since 10:30 p.m. the night Brooke disappeared that someone who represented themselves to be the kidnappers had contacted the Hart family by telephone: "The voice was smooth, softly accusatory—the voice a schoolteacher might use with a recalcitrant pupil" (p. 63).

> "You didn't follow orders, Mr. Hart. You did not drive

> south. You did not follow the instructions we gave Charlie O'Brien. Why not, Mr. Hart?"
>
> "I'll do anything to get my boy back, but I need some proof that you really have him."
>
> "Look, I can tell you exactly what your son was wearing when we took him. He had on an overcoat, and a light felt hat, and he was carrying his glasses. That hasn't been in the newspapers" (p. 64).

Swift Justice noted that no mention of the coat, hat, or glasses had ever been made in the newspapers.

> "[Alex Hart] Can you give me a sample of his handwriting, or one of his shoes, or something else he was carrying?"
>
> "Brooke is a long way from San Jose. This is your last chance, Mr. Hart. You still have time to catch the 9:30 train to Los Angeles. Catch it and the man in the white mask will meet you. When the money is turned over, your boy will be released in the morning. Take that train…or it will be too bad" (p. 64).

The call was traced to a downtown San Jose garage where an attendant had seen a man use the pay phone:

> "Ruddy-faced about five-feet eleven. 160 pounds. Pretty well dressed—light brown overcoat and light grey hat" (p. 65).

The sheriff and FBI agents took the parking attendant with them and staked out the Southern Pacific train depot in San Jose. The FBI mistook a bank teller out for an evening stroll as the ransom caller, and jumped from their cars with guns drawn. Terrified, the man ran and was tackled. Sheriff Emig, who knew the teller, intervened to get him released (p. 66).

In shambles was the cover story given to the newspapers that law enforcement had pulled back from the kidnap investigation at the request of Alex Hart.

Third Ransom Letter

The third ransom letter, postmarked in San Jose on Wednesday, November 15th arrived at L. Hart & Son early the same afternoon:

> *"YOU WANT MORE PROOF. MR. HART, THIS IS NOT A BUSINESS TRANSACTION. THIS IS A KIDNAPPING WITH EVERY AVAILABLE RESOURCE OF AID AT YOUR SERVICE. ANY THIRD PARTY CONTACT WITH US IS PERSONAL SUICIDE. IN SHORT, YOU DON'T TRUST US WE DON'T TRUST YOU, SO FURTHER DISCUSSION IS USELESS.*
>
> *"WE HOLD THE CARDS IN THIS CASE. BROOKE IS NOT WITH THE WRITER BUT IT HELD AT A REMOTE POINT. WHEN PAYMENTIS MADE A TELEGRAM BY CONTACING PARTIES WILL RELEASE BROOKE. BROOKE IS BEING TREATED WELL AS POSSIBLE BUT THE CASE IS GETTING TOO MUCH PUBLICITY FOR US TO HOLD HIM ANY LONGER. WE ARE SORRY TO DO THIS BECAUSE BROOKE IS A MANLY LAD, BUT HE HAS SEEN US AND IS TOO LIABLE TO IDENTIFY US.*
>
> *"KILLING HIM IS THE EASY WAY WITH LITTLE RISK FOR US. RETURNING HIM IS WHAT WE DEMANDED THE RANSOM FOR. SORRY, I CAN'T GET SOME FURTHER PROOF FOR YOU BUT I SAID THE WRITER IS THE CONTACT MAN ONLY.*

WE DO NOT HOLD BROOKE HART HERE. MR. HART, UNLESS OUR PRINCIPALS HEAR FAVORABLY FROM US BY 7:30 11-15-33 YOU WILL NOT BE CONTACTED AGAIN. IT WILL BE USELESS. IF YOU COMPLY TO OUR DEMANDS PUT A NUMERAL TWO WHERE THE 1 IS NOW IS AS SOON AS IT IS RECEIVED. STARTING 7:30 P.M. 11-15-33 DRIVE SOUTH ON MONTERERY ROAD TO LOS ANGELES. TAKE MALIBU HIGHWAY INTO L.A.

"IF YOU ARE NOT STOPPED BEFORE L.A. STOP AT THE MAYFAIR HOTEL OVER NIGHT W. SEVENTH STREET, L.A. RETURN 7:30 P.M. SAME ROUTE AS BEFORE. FOLLOWING NIGHT HAVE RUMBLE SEAT OPEN AT ALL TIMES. BAG WITH CURRENCY BESIDE YOU AND YOUR FAMILY WILL NOT BE MOLESTED FURTHER BY US OR ANY OTHER ORGANIZATION. FAIL US—YOU LOSE AS SON AAS WELL AS THE $40,000 BECAUSE YOU ARE SLATED TO MAKE THIS PAYMENT IRREGARDLESS.

"SEE TO IT THAT YOU ARE NOT FOLLOWED AND THIS TIME START AT 7:30 P.M. IN STUDE ROADSTER. THIS IS THE LAST CONTACT UNTIL YOU MEET THE MAN WITH THE WHITE MASK. DO NOT TRAVEL OVER 10 MP.H. BE SURE YOU ARE ALONE."[6]

The recommendation of the FBI was to place the numeral (2) in the store window as demanded, but add the words: "I CANNOT DRIVE."

---

[6] FBI File

At 7:20 p.m., FBI Special Agent Ramsey, secreted in the Hart mansion, received a telephone call from the chief operator of the phone company:

> "Two calls have been placed to the Hart home, Ballard 2013, in the past eight minutes. Each time the calling party hung up before we could ring the number" (p. 73).

The calls from San Jose came from the Montgomery Hotel at First and San Antonio Streets, and Tuggle's Drug Store at Tenth and Santa Clara Streets.

Fourth Ransom Call

Just before eight o'clock, telephones jangled at the Hart mansion. Alex Hart picked one up:

> "Is Mr. Hart there?"

> "It was the smooth, soft male voice that both Alex and Miriam had described" (p. 74).

As the caller hectored Alex Hart about the ransom payment, the operator revealed on another line that the call was being made from a pay phone in the Plaza garage, 150 feet from San Jose Police headquarters.

Sheriff Emig and the FBI agents arrived at the garage and spotted a man with his back to them as he talked on the pay phone. As Emig and the agents closed in, the man placed the earpiece back into its cradle:

> "He was a thin-faced, ruddy young man with large ears and brown wavy hair receding at the temples. A two-day stubble of dark beard covered his chin. He wore

corduroy trousers with high topped boots and an old dark-blue sweater. ‘What’s your name, mister?’ Emig demanded.”

“Harold Thurmond” (p. 77).

Part III The Confessions

Taken into custody a little after 8:00 p.m., Thurmond was interrogated hour after hour by Sheriff Emig, San Jose Police Chief J.N. Black, FBI special agents, and political boss, attorney Louis Oneal:

> "The officers wanted to get Thurmond's signature on the document [confession], before he had the opportunity to secure legal counsel" (p.118).

Thurmond attested that he had made his confession voluntarily, although there was appropriate suspicion that it was the product of hours of third degree at a time when Miranda warnings were only in the imagination of the American criminal defense bar.

Thurmond informed his interrogators that his fellow kidnapper and murderer, Jack Holmes, had moved to the California Hotel three days previously after he had separated from his wife. Holmes was arrested in his room at approximately 3:30 a.m.

Analysis

The acceptance of the confessions at "face value" in *Swift Justice* provides a useful structure for the analysis and comparison of the statements of salient facts confessed by Thurmond and Holmes.

Everything in the confessions, except for statements about what had transpired when the two men were alone, was derived from either the record of ransom calls and written demands, or extrapolated from previously acquired information held confidential by law enforcement. Since there were no eyewitnesses—save for Delphine and Isabelle Silveria whose verified accounts were later publicly dismissed by both the sheriff and the FBI—evidence was required to corroborate the admissions that Thurmond and Holmes had made in their confessions.

In confessions in which each suspect blames the other, statements of fact must be independently corroborated to be admissible in a court of law.

Absent corroborative evidence, the content of these confessions would have allowed the authorities to charge literally anyone, simply through the insertion of their name, with the kidnapping and murder of Brooke Hart.

The uncorroborated confessions proved more than sufficient, however, to convict Holmes and Thurmond in the court of public opinion.

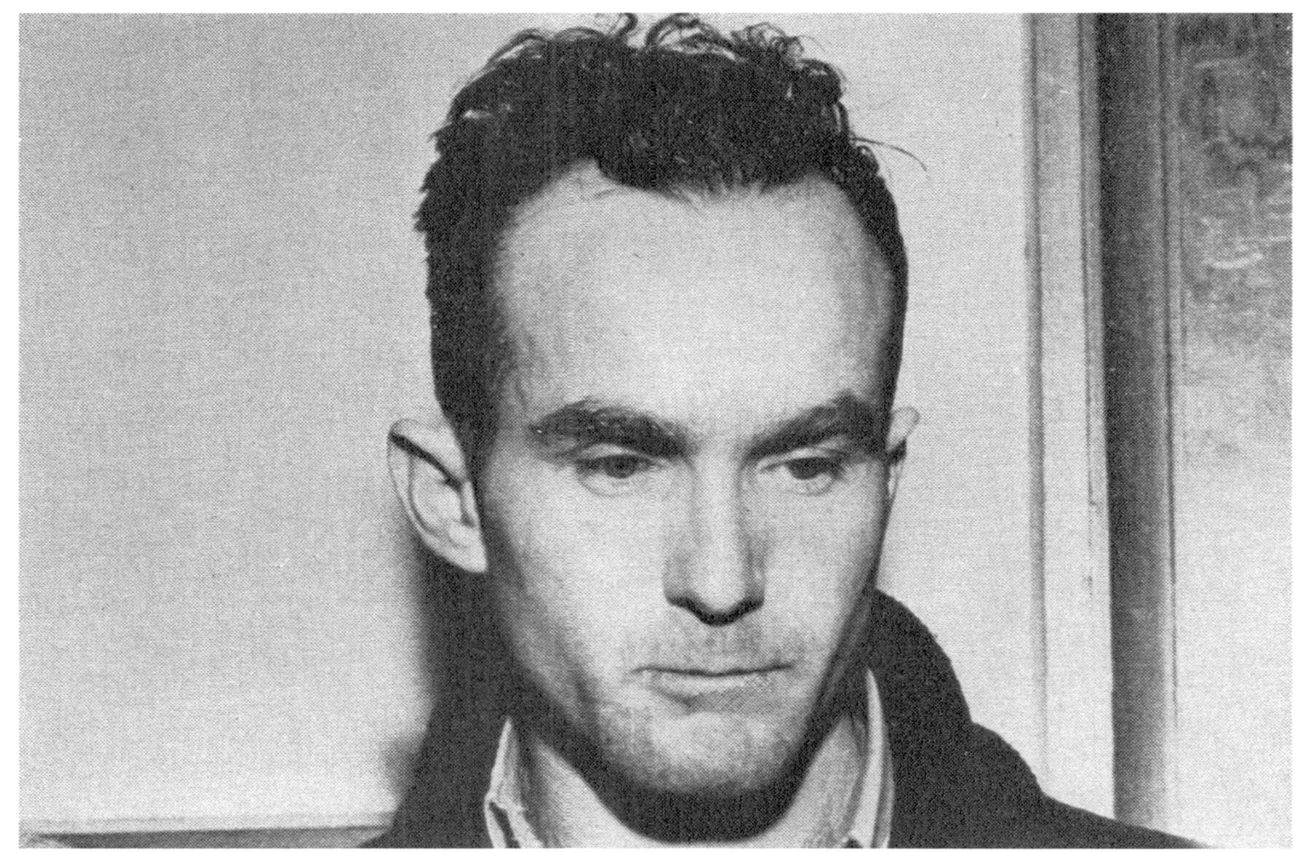

Photo of Thomas Thurmond taken in San Jose jail short time before lynching – *Courtesy of the Bancroft Library, University of California, Berkeley*

Thurmond's Confession:[7]

Statement:	"We discussed this matter on one or two occasions and on Thursday November 9, 1933, shortly before six o'clock p.m. [sic], Jack Holmes and I saw Brooke Hart come toward the parking lot where he used to park his Studebaker roadster."
Source:	Hart family members and the parking lot attendant stated that Brooke Hart went to the parking lot to get his car to take his father to a meeting on or around 6 o'clock in the evening. The attendant recalled that Brooke stopped at the exit to the lot about to turn right on Market Street.
Statement:	"Brooke Hart obtained his car…and drove out the driveway toward Market Street. Jack Holmes met the car of Brooke Hart at the curb and opened the door…with one hand and had the other in his pocket as though he had a gun."
Source:	Thurmond's uncorroborated statement. Such a scenario was plausible for anyone who might have committed the crime.
Statement:	"Jack Holmes and Brooke Hart drove by in the latter's Studebaker roadster to a point on Evans Road about seven to ten miles from San Jose."
Source:	Brooke Hart's Studebaker was seen on Evans Road at 7:00 p.m. by the wife of the manager

---

[7] FBI File

of the San Jose Country Club.

Statement: "When Jack Holmes stopped the Brooke Hart Studebaker…they both got out of the car and Jack Holmes told Brooke Hart to get in the back of the Chevrolet coach I was driving."

Source: Thurmond's uncorroborated statement. Both Holmes and Thurmond claimed they used Holmes's car with license plates that identified him as the registered owner.

Statement: "I was sitting at the right of Jack Holmes when he was driving the car. We then turned north and drove through Irvington and Alvarado and then direct to the San Mateo Bridge."

Source: The Studebaker was found abandoned on Evans Road. At approximately 7:25 p.m. that night, two wood-gatherers reported that someone called for help on the San Mateo Bridge.

Statement: "We stopped about half a mile out on the San Mateo bridge at which time Brooke Hart was ordered out of the car and Jack Holmes walked back of the car—to the rear of Brooke Hart's car [sic] and hit him over the head with a brick which I had obtained at a cement company in San Jose… .

"When Jack Holmes hit Brooke Hart over the head with this brick he hollered 'help, help,' but Jack Holmes hit him over the head again with the brick and knocked Brooke Hart unconscious."

Source: Thurmond's uncorroborated statement which

blamed Holmes for the physical assault on Brooke Hart (see: Holmes's confession).

Statement: "I took some bailing wire. . . . and bound the arms of Brooke Hart around his body up close to his shoulders."

Source: Thurmond's uncorroborated statement (see: Holmes's confession).

Statement: "Jack Holmes then told me to take hold of him—Jack Holmes took hold of the upper part of Brooke Hart's body and I took hold of him from his knees down and together we lifted him onto the railing of the San Mateo Bridge. I recall as we lifted him. . . . he struggled slightly."

Source**:** Thurmond's uncorroborated statement (see: Holmes's confession).

Statement: "We then turned around in the Chevrolet coach and returned to San Jose, California.

"I kept the wallet [Brooke Hart's], in my possession.

"After we returned to San Jose. . . I returned to San Francisco in my father's machine, a Pontiac car, and . . . I was to . . . throw the wallet into the bay."

Source: Thurmond's uncorroborated account, ransom calls traced to San Francisco, and the discovery of the wallet by the deckhand.

Statement: "I was also to telephone Mr. Hart…advising him that his son was kidnapped and being held for $40,000 ransom.

"I endeavored to put a call through from a place, I believe on Market Street, but the line was busy. I first tried to place the telephone call about 9:30 p.m. on November 9, 1933.

"I then placed another long distance call. Some man answered the telephone and I inquired for Mr. Hart and then some girl answered the phone and I told her that her brother was being held…and if the family notified the police that they would never see Brooke Hart again."

Source: Telephone trace on Hart home telephone, and recollections of FBI agents and Miriam Hart.

Statement: "I walked down the waterfront for two or three blocks and tossed the wallet into the San Francisco Bay."

Source: The wallet discovered by the deckhand.

Statement: "On November 10th, 1933 . . . I left in my father's Pontiac car for Sacramento, California. Jack Holmes had already given me a card with a message for Mr. Hart."

Source: First ransom card with a Sacramento, California postmark.

Statement: "Jack Holmes gave me a letter to take to San Francisco to mail to Mr. Hart. The letter was printed by Jack Holmes. I was watching Jack Holmes when he wrote the letter and read the same which specified that Mr. Hart place the numeral (1) in the window of his store. . . if he was willing to proceed with further negotiations."

Source: Thurmond's uncorroborated statement, and contents of the second ransom letter.

Statement: "I drove to San Francisco in my father's car…and I mailed the letter to Mr. Hart."

Source: The San Francisco postmark on the second ransom letter.

Statement: "Jack Holmes and I both went by Hart's store Tuesday November 14, 1933, and both saw the numeral (1) in the window."

"Jack Holmes called Charlie O'Brien, a personal friend of Brooke Hart's . . . , and gave... message to deliver to Mr. Hart."

Source**:** Thurmond's uncorroborated statement, and record of telephone call to Charlie O'Brien.

Statement: "Mr. Hart was to take a satchel with $40,000 in it and place same on the seat. . . and drive in Brooke Hart's Studebaker roadster toward Los Angeles."

Source: Charlie O'Brien's recollection of the ransom call instructions.

Statement: "About 8:45 p.m., I telephoned Mr. Hart from a pay station at Perry's parking lot at [sic] San Jose. I asked Mr. Hart why he had not kept his previous appointment and he told me he wanted further proof that we were holding his son, Brooke Hart."

Source: The record of the ransom call.

Statement: "On November 15, 1933, Jack Holmes printed another letter. . . . He also addressed the envelope and mailed this letter in the post office to Mr. Hart in which letter [sic] we advised Mr. Hart there had been some confusion…and outlined to him the telephone [sic] from San Francisco and the card from Sacramento together with the letter in regard to placing the numeral (1) in the window and told him there had been too much publicity, but if Mr. Hart was willing to go through with the negotiations…he was to place the numeral (2)... in his window."

Source: Written ransom demands.

Statement: "About 7:12 p.m. [sic] of November 15, 1933, we drove the car in the vicinity of the Montgomery Hotel and Jack Holmes endeavored to get in touch with Mr. Hart through a pay telephone.

"We then drove to Tuggle's drug store. . . and Jack Holmes again tried to get in touch with Mr. Hart at 7:19 p.m."

Source: Thurmond's uncorroborated statement; records of telephone trace.

Statement: "We then went to Sabbatte Brothers garage at 222 South Market Street, and I telephoned Mr. Hart from a pay station in the rear end of the garage. About the time I was finished with the call, I was taken into custody by Sheriff Emig."

Source: Record of telephone call; report of Thurmond's arrest.

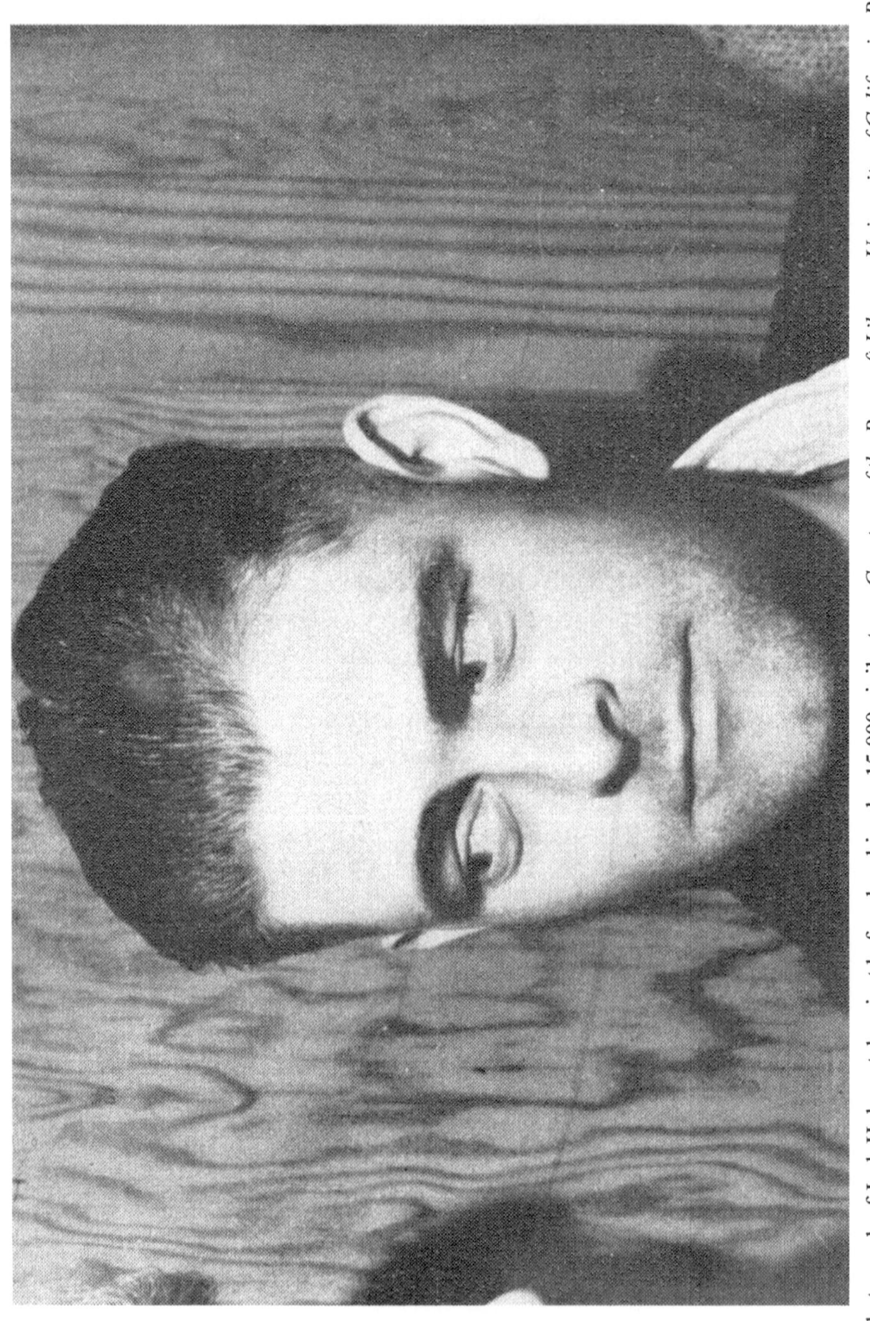

Jail photograph of Jack Holmes taken just before lynching by 15,000 vigilantes – *Courtesy of the Bancroft Library, University of California, Berkeley*

Holmes's Confession[8]

Statement:	"I have known Harold Thurmond for about one year."
	"A couple of days before this kidnapping, in fact it was the day before—no, I guess it was about two days before. . .he grabbed me by the arm,. . .. and says, 'There goes Brooke Hart—if we. . . pick him up we could get a piece of change out of him.'"
Source:	Thurmond's confession. Holmes blamed the kidnap idea on Thurmond; neither statement can be corroborated.
***Statement*:**	"We pulled up there [Hart's store] at 3 o'clock and stopped. We drove there on the 8th of November, and we waited there."
Source:	Holmes's uncorroborated statement.
***Statement*:**	"We sat there until 6 o'clock . . . this fellow Brooke Hart and his dad came out."
	"I asked. . . 'where would he keep the boy in the event we picked him up?' 'Not that I know except that you might put him on a boat or something.' Then I said, 'Harold that would be foolish; I can't be away from home anyway.'"
	"We talked it over…Harold said, Yes you know the smart thing is to dump that guy overboard some place. "

[8] FBI File

Source:	Holmes's uncorroborated statement.
Statement:	"Then I met him at 5 o'clock the next evening just before I was going home." "I asked him if he knew Brooke Hart—'I have seen him at various times and was able to identify him.'" "He said, 'You will have to take him in his own car, as he will recognize me.' " "I said, 'The only place to take this guy to quiz him is on some back road.' So Harold agreed to meet me on the Calaveras Road in my car."
Source:	Thurmond's uncorroborated statements. Eyewitness who had identified Brooke Hart's Studebaker in Milpitas.
Statement:	"So I walked over to the edge of the sidewalk by his car—by the telephone building and waited for him. . . and I climbed on the running board and had my hand in my pocket like that. And stuck my fingers against his ribs."
Source:	Thurmond's uncorroborated statement; recollection of parking attendant of Brooke Hart's car at Market Street exit.
Statement:	"I then drove him out to Milpitas. I turned left on Post Street going down to San Pedro, turned right on Julian, down Julian to thirteenth to Milpitas. I had arranged beforehand to meet Harold in Milpitas."
Source:	Thurmond's uncorroborated statement. Eyewitness account of Brooke Hart's car abandoned in Milpitas.

Statement: "Harold said, 'If we dump this guy and write a note and get a quick turnover before they get too worried.' "

"I said, 'how are you going to tie him up?' and he said, 'we will tie him up before we get out of the car.' And I said, 'All right if you think you can handle it.' "

Source: Thurmond's and Holmes's uncorroborated statements.

Statement: "When we got to the San Mateo Bridge and by the draw there was [sic] no cars around, and Harold ordered Hart out of the car, and he got out and didn't know where he was because he had this pillow slip over his head."

Source: Holmes's uncorroborated statement.

Statement: "We led him to believe he was going to be transferred from one machine to another,. . . and a car came by and he [Hart], started to shout, and I hauled off and hit him with my fist. I guess he hit his head on the concrete as he fell as he laid quite still for a few moments."

Source: Holmes's uncorroborated statement..

Statement: "Then Harold reached into the car and got the wire and started wrapping his feet and his hands, and at that time he passed me the gun."

Source: Thurmond's uncorroborated statement.

Statement: "Harold got the two concrete blocks and tied them around his feet and we tossed him overboard."

Source: Holmes's uncorroborated statement.

Statement: "After that I don't know what it was. . . he [Hart], made some sound and fanned around and Harold said, "'Give me the gun,'" and he climbed down the stringers [sic] and fired the cartridges. . . where he imagined Hart would be."

Source: Report of wood gatherers to Hayward police; Thurmond's and Holmes's uncorroborated statements.

Statement: "While he was doing that I drove up the bridge a ways and turned around and came back. I looked for Harold on the same side of the bridge he had gone down on but finally saw him on the other side of the bridge. . . . when he got into the car I asked him what happened and Harold said 'I am not sure,…but I don't think he will ever come up again.' "

Source: Thurmond's and Holmes's uncorroborated statements.

Statement: "[Sheriff Emig] 'What time did he phone [Hart residence] about 10:30?' "

"[Holmes] 'Yes that would be about right.'"

"[Sheriff Emig] 'Just what was the arrangement about the telephoning?'"

"[Holmes] 'We decided…that we should demand $40,000. Harold went to San Francisco and I went home.' "

Source: Record of ransom demands and call content; Thurmond's and Holmes's uncorroborated statements.

Statement: "We agreed to meet Monday, the 13th, and the card was written stating our demands, and Harold mailed it from Sacramento that night."

"[Sheriff Emig] 'Who wrote the card?' "

"[Holmes] 'The first one we both wrote.' "

Source: Ransom notes; Thurmond's and Holmes's uncorroborated statements.

Statement: "The second note was written directing Mr. Hart to drive south on the Los Angeles highway with the currency."

Source: Ransom notes and calls; Thurmond's and Holmes's uncorroborated statements.

Statement: "We made several phone calls but realized we were being checked on and left without contacting Mr. Hart."

Source: Record of telephone trace on Hart telephone; Thurmond's and Holmes's uncorroborated statements.

Statement: "The last phone call was from the Plaza garage, where Harold went in to use the telephone while I was parked opposite Burke's garage waiting for him. That was the last I saw of him."

Source: Telephone trace; record of ransom call; Thurmond's and Holmes's uncorroborated statements.

Contradictions in the Confessions

- Thurmond confessed that the kidnapping was Holmes's idea; Holmes confessed that it was Thurmond's.
- Thurmond confessed that he first saw Brooke Hart on November 9th, the day of the kidnapping; Holmes confessed that they first saw Hart on November 8th.
- Holmes confessed that he met Thurmond at 5:00 p.m. on November 9th ; Thurmond confessed that they met at 6:00 p.m.
- Thurmond confessed that they stopped one half mile out from the eastern toll entrance on the San Mateo Bridge; Holmes confessed that they stopped by the drawbridge some three and one half miles out.
- Thurmond confessed that Holmes hit Brooke Hart twice on the head with a twenty-two pound concrete block; Holmes confessed that he hit him with his fist.
- Holmes confessed that Thurmond tied concrete blocks to Hart's feet; Thurmond confessed that he bound him with wire.
- Holmes confessed that Thurmond climbed under the bridge, and fired gunshots at Hart; Thurmond did not confess that he had either climbed under the bridge, or fired a gun.
- Thurmond confessed that he and Holmes agreed to toss Hart's wallet in the bay; Holmes did not confess to anything about the wallet.

- Thurmond confessed that he met with Holmes on Friday November 10th , Saturday November11th, and Monday November 13th. Holmes confessed that he met with Thurmond on November 11th, 14th, and 15th.

- Thurmond confessed that he received the first ransom note from Holmes on November 10th. Holmes confessed that he provided the note on November 13th, and that Thurmond mailed it from Sacramento that night.

- Thurmond confessed that he got the second ransom note from Holmes on November 11th. Holmes confessed that he wrote the second ransom note on November 14th, and gave it to Thurmond.

Holmes confessed that he had ordered Thurmond to make the ransom call from the garage that resulted in his capture, and had parked his Chevrolet facing the entrance to wait for him. It was the same garage where Holmes, as a new resident of the California Hotel next door, kept his car. *Swift Justice* speculated on his muddled thoughts:

> "From his vantage point . . . Jack should have seen Sheriff Emig enter the building seven minutes later. He should have noticed the business-suited and felt-hatted FBI agents racing down the sidewalk from the St. Claire Hotel. Whatever the reason, all the danger signals escaped him. When Harold had been gone more than a phone call ought to take, Jack circled the block a couple of times, and then drove aimlessly around the city" (p. 111).

Swift Justice also imagined the machinations of Holmes's conscience:

> "Now was the moment for him to fall back on

> whatever escape plan his scenario called for. But brash Jack Holmes never considered the eventuality of failure; there was no plan. His cunning and caution had failed under the overload of a lost job, a lost family, frustrated sexual fantasies, and his secret career as a desperado" (p.111).

But finally, an hour after Thurmond had been arrested, despite Holmes's apparently terminal existential angst, he parked his car in the same garage, exchanged cheerful banter with the attendant, had dinner at a nearby tavern, and went to bed (p.111). Holmes had made no effort to determine what had happened to Harold Thurmond.

The garage attendant had described Holmes as a "jaunty figure in a light blue suit and a panama hat" (p. 111). Holmes's manner, appearance, and behavior suggest that he had been out socializing rather than waiting anxiously for the outcome of the ransom negotiations handled by his foil Thurmond.

Public Reaction

Because of the sheer horror of the acts to which both Thurmond and Holmes had confessed, discrepancies in the confessions were both ignored or dismissed out-of-hand. The public revulsion over the dispassionate admission, by two brazen opportunists out for a quick buck, about the brutal execution of an innocent young man established the foundation of fact that resulted—with the complicity of the powers-that-be and the press—in the lynching of Thurmond and Holmes.

In San Jose, California, in 1933, as well as the rest of the nation, people were largely unaccustomed to, and unfamiliar with, the graphic, stomach-turning depictions of human violence that have dominated both the news and entertainment media over the last forty years. In 1933, such violent human on human imagery shocked people deeply, and the emotional response, unlike in the modern day, was not desensitized or hardened:

> "Grief hung like a pall over Hart's Department Store. Of the two hundred employees, their movements were automatic, their speech subdued, their throats tight from holding back emotion. Many wept openly, and were not ashamed" (p. 172).

The citizens of San Jose read and gossiped about two greedy home-town miscreants who stupidly kidnapped, on a street where most people would know them, the high profile son of a respected family. Barely one and a half hours later, his skull was bashed twice with a twenty-two pound concrete block. He was then bound hand and foot, and tossed into the San Francisco Bay. When it appeared that he was still alive, one shot at him repeatedly from under the bridge.

The horror and enormity of such acts shook the people of San Jose to their core:

> "The word of the murder fell like a thunderbolt, and on the heels of the stunned realization came a wave of intense anger. Groups collected in the street. Their faces grim. In step with the anger marched fear, lust for vengeance, jitters, sullen suspicion, and paranoia" (p. 170).

Their revulsion was amplified when it was learned that Jack Holmes met his wife shortly after he murdered Brooke Hart, and then went to the movies with friends to share laughter as they watched Disney's *Three Little Pigs*. It was heightened by subsequent accounts of Holmes's friendliness and jocularity as he went about his daily life, while at the same time, he allegedly orchestrated the extortion of ransom with the false and terribly cruel hope that the kidnap victim he murdered would be returned unharmed to his family.

Further outrage arose from reports that Thurmond had been seen next to his mother at church on the Sunday between the kidnapping, murder, and his arrest.

Following the arrests, daily press accounts relentlessly stoked San Jose's rage. Many people truly believed that Holmes and Thurmond were the "Human Devils," described in an editorial published in the *San Jose News*.

As evidenced by the leadership role soon to be taken by the then governor of California, it was a foregone conclusion that the men were guilty, and destined to pay the ultimate price for their crimes.

Such extraordinary violence, brutal callousness, and craven greed obviated the need for a trial; no jury in the world would fail to convict two such men and recommend the death sentence.

Unfortunately for Thurmond and Holmes, the confessions that convicted them in the court of public opinion were factually wrong, grossly misinterpreted, and cynically devised.

Principal Discrepancies

Abandoned Studebaker

The wife of the manager of the San Jose Country Club stated that she first saw a car abandoned with its headlights on near her home at 7:00 p.m. the night of the kidnapping.

Delphine and Isabelle Silveria had witnessed five men and the "light-haired driver" of the Studebaker stop some thirty feet from their barn at 6:30 p.m. on the night of the kidnapping. They lived a mile and a half south from where the Studebaker was abandoned. They were the only eyewitnesses to the Brooke Hart kidnapping.

Their description of the car matched that of the vehicle observed repeatedly in the alley next to L. Hart & Son over the ten days prior to the kidnapping, but not afterwards.

Verification of the Eyewitness Accounts

Three days prior to the arrests of Thurmond and Holmes, Sheriff Emig and the FBI went to elaborate lengths to prove or disprove the recollections of the mother and daughter. A detailed account of the verification process together with the findings of fact is contained in the FBI file on the Brooke L. Hart kidnapping.

On November 15, 1933, FBI Special Agent in Charge Reed Vetterli filed a written report to J. Edgar Hoover [9] that contained the eyewitnesses' accounts, and the process employed to verify their recollections:

---

[9] FBI File

“One Mrs. Silveria, residing in San Jose, outlined particular circumstances which indicate possible kidnapping of Brooke L. Hart from his Studebaker roadster to a large sedan, about 7:00 P.M., November 9, 1933.

“About 11:00 A.M., Monday, November 13, a Mrs. Silveria…called on the sheriff's office where she was interviewed by agents and Sheriff Emig. Mrs. Silveria…stated that on Thursday night, about 6:30 or 7:00 P.M., while she…was out in her yard…with her daughter Isabelle… could see lights coming from the distance, and she wondered if it could make the turn a 100 yards away, which is on the Piedmont Road. The automobile was a dark, large sedan. She does not know the make, but stated that it had a very long hood from the radiator to the windshield. The car pulled along a ditch up the roadway, which leads up around the hills, and which, if continued for a mile and a half, reaches the point where the car of young Brooke Hart was later found abandoned.

“Directly following the large dark sedan was a roadster, and this roadster pulled up back of the dark sedan opposite Mrs. Silveria's barn. On each side of the roadster was a man standing on the running board, and…one man was heard to say” ‘We got him all right’.” Then someone commanded the driver to get out of the roadster, and stated: “’Get in there big boy,’” and then someone is heard to say “’Are we on the right road?’”[sic] and then someone else said “’You hit this road into Milpitas, and then on to Oakland Road.’” Then one man said ’Where are we going from here?’ Another said [sic] ’We are going to head for Stockton, and then shoot to Sacramento …. Then another man said ’What about the gas’ [sic] and the other said ’The tank is full,’ and some other said ‘What about the

> license plates' [sic], and someone replied [sic]'Leave it as it is.'"
>
> "She stated she heard a rattling noise like tin in the back of the car. They then started with their lights out, one man getting into the roadster, and driving off rapidly, and four men, in addition to some unknown party, driving off in the large, dark sedan. She stated that they drove off very rapidly, and she could hear the sound of their motors for some distance. All in all, Mrs. Silveria saw five men, in addition to the man taken out of the roadster. She called attention to the fact that the roadster had some sort of canvas top, and stated that the man taken out of the roadster did not make any remarks whatsoever, but was wearing a light felt hat, and light overcoat, and from what she could see, a light gray suit. This tallies with the clothing worn by Hart.
>
> "She stated that the men apparently conversed in good English, and did not appear to be foreigners, although, of course, she could not describe them. She got a better view of the two cars, namely the sedan and the roadster, when they were parked, when the darker car drove down the road, and the lights furnished a clearer vision."

To affirm Mrs. Silveria's account, Special Agent Vetterli and Sheriff Emig located her daughter, Isabelle, at school, and interviewed her before she could discuss what she had seen with her mother.

> "Before Mrs. Silveria could again talk with her daughter, Isabelle Silveria, who was with her this night near the barn, Agents and Sheriff Emig located Isabelle Silveria at a local school in San Jose, and questioned her. She stated that she and her mother were going to

> the lavoratory about 6:30 P.M, after dinner. She would place the time about 6:30 because they always have dinner at 6:00 o'clock, she stated that right after dinner, she saw two cars draw up in front of her barn…one a black sedan, the other a roadster with a canvas top. She claims she saw five men in all, and heard them talk about "plates" but does not know what they meant. She can't remember the conversation in detail, but describes what took place the same as Mrs. Silveria.
>
> "With regard to fixing the date, Mrs. Silveria states…they have no water on their place, and accordingly…goes to her sisters to wash clothes. They do not get any newspapers at home, and she remembers specifically that it was the day following the night she saw this incident that she was at her sister's washing clothes when she heard about the Hart kidnapping. And this would positively place the night as November 9th, about 6:30."

The evening following the independent interviews with Mrs. Silveria and her daughter, the agents and the sheriff staged a test near their farm to help determine whether their recollection was both possible and accurate.

> "On Monday night, the 13th, in company with Sheriff Emig, Agent's took Brooke Hart's car, and Agent's car, which is also a coupe of a darker color, and drove out to the home of Mrs. Silveria, and placed the two cars in the exact position where she stated the sedan and roadster were placed, and while these cars are about twenty-five or thirty feet away from Mrs. Silveria was [sic] talking in ordinary conversational tones can be distinctly heard from the cars to the point where Mrs. Silveria was located. The acoustic properties at that time of night are splendid, and one

can hear distinctly ordinary conversation.

> "We did not tell Mrs. Silveria the roadster was the car belonging to the Victim [sic] Brooke Hart. However, she stated without any prompting and pointing to Hart's car "That looks like the roadster there." At that particular time of night Mrs. Silveria and her daughter could have readily seen the transaction as described. Complete tests were made by placing men at the point where the cars were, in both light and dark suits, and the coloring could be discerned. In addition, we could tell that one was darker than the other. Hence, it appears that Mrs. Silveria is correct in her version."

> "Close questioning of Mrs. Silveria indicated that she was not endeavoring to furnish any fabricated story, but was apparently telling the truth, and she appeared sincere and genuine in relating the incident in question, and efforts were made to confuse her slightly to if, per chance, she were not telling the truth, but she sticks splendidly to her story. She stated that her daughter…would have liked to call Sheriff Emig, believing that they were probably bootleggers, but of course they had no phone in their home."

In 1987, *Swift Justice* author Harry Farrell contacted the sixty-eight-year-old Isabelle Silveria:

> "She instantly recalled the 1933 episode with clarity and related her experience anew, without essential change from what she and her mother had reported fifty-four years earlier. For the author, she later drew a detailed map pinpointing the locations of the two cars and the positions of her mother and herself in relation to their house, their barn, and the road" (p. 285).

Eight days after the arrest of Holmes and Thurmond, rather than five men seen one half hour after the kidnapping, U.S. Attorney H. H. McPike informed reporters of the Silveria's eyewitness accounts (p. 178). Both Emig and the FBI had kept the account confidential:

> "[Sheriff] Emig was furious. Now he dug his heels in deeper than ever on his assertion that Holmes and Thurmond had acted by themselves. He belittled Mrs. Silveria as an unreliable observer" (p. 178).

Special Agent in Charge Vetterli also denigrated the veracity of Mrs. Silveria's eyewitness account:

> "I place little credence in Mrs. Silveria's story. It has been completely checked, and we could find nothing to it" (p. 178).

Vetterli's statement factually contradicted what he had documented in his written report to J. Edgar Hoover after he verified the mother's and daughter's eyewitness accounts. The FBI Brooke Hart kidnapping file also contains a facsimile of the telegram Vetterli sent to J. Edgar Hoover on the night of November 13, 1933 after the eyewitness verifications:

> *"DEVELOPMENTS TODAY INDICATE HART KIDNAPPED BY FIVE MEN DRIVING A LARGE BLACK SEDAN BEARING CALIFORNIA LICENSE."*

In comparison to the long-hooded "large sedan" identified in the eyewitness accounts, Jack Holmes drove a black 1933 two-door Chevrolet coach.

It was not until fifty years later when the Brooke L. Hart kidnapping file was made public under the Freedom of Information Act, that this incendiary contradiction finally became public.

The FBI summary report on the kidnapping does not contain the eyewitness accounts of Delphine and Isabelle Silveria.

Brooke Hart's Wallet

Thurmond confessed that after the 10:30 ransom call to the Hart family, he had walked down Market Street in San Francisco from the Witcomb Hotel to the Embarcadero, then south to Pier 32 where he had tossed Brooke Hart's wallet into the bay. Thurmond then had walked back to where he had parked his father's Pontiac near the speakeasy where he had tried, but failed, to make the initial ransom call at 9:30, and drove back to San Jose where he arrived about midnight.

Whether Thurmond's confession is taken at "face value" (as in *Swift Justice),* or assessed by objective fact, he could not have thrown Brooke Hart's wallet into the bay.

The oil tanker began to fuel the cruise ship at midnight, and the guardrail of the fuel tanker did not rise above the waterline until later in the morning when sufficient weight of the fuel had been pumped out. To land onto the guardrail, Hart's wallet had to have been thrown after the guardrail showed. The wallet was only damp inside, and therefore had landed on the guardrail after someone tossed it, rather than having floated onto it from the water.

Thurmond confessed that he had tossed the wallet between 10:30 and 11:00 p.m. on the night of the kidnapping. At the time he tossed the wallet off Pier 32, the oil tanker guardrail was still under the water. During the only window of time the wallet could have had been thrown to land on the guardrail, Thurmond confessed he was in San Jose.

Jack Holmes's Alibi Chain

Jack Holmes confessed that he had met Thurmond at 5:00 p.m., November 9th, the night of the kidnapping. Thurmond confessed that he met Holmes at 6:00 p.m. that night.

While Holmes's confession stated that Thurmond joined him in his car around 5:00 p.m., the night of the kidnapping, statements of his alibi witnesses cast material doubt on its factual accuracy.

Alibi One

At 5:00 p.m. the night of the kidnapping, Jack Holmes rang the doorbell at the home of Harvey and Ruth Gum who lived on the southern city limits of San Jose. Ruth Gum answered the door, and let Jack Holmes inside where they chatted "until not long before 6:00 p.m." (p. 150).

Ruth Gum and her husband appeared at the sheriff's office to make a statement. She was certain that Holmes had been there between five and six, but could not recall exactly when he had left.

Alibi Two

Evelyn Holmes, Jack's wife, spoke with a district attorney investigator:

> "Evelyn told him it would be utterly impossible that Jack could have had anything to do with the Hart case. During the critical hours of Brooke's disappearance and ostensible murder . . . he had been with her at home" (p. 129).

Alibi Three

Hulda Holmes, Jack Holmes's mother, stated that she was with Jack and Evelyn at their home the night of the kidnapping:

> "I was over at my son's house that night; his wife had helped fit a dress for me. He was as sweet as he always was. He wasn't under any strain. I'm his mother and would know if there was anything wrong with him, which there wasn't" (p. 137).

Alibi Four

Maurice Holmes, Jack Holmes's well-respected father, declared:

> "Our boy is innocent—innocent I tell you. We know where he was that night. I can prove almost every minute of it" (p. 245).

> "[*Swift Justice*] The 'proof' rested on his steadfast insistence that it only had been seven o'clock on the kidnapping night when Jack arrived home to pick up Evelyn for their movie date with the Estensen's" (p. 245).

> "[Maurice Holmes] We can prove the stories of that man Thurmond were lies. They forced my boy to confess something he never did. My boy was only accused by one man, Thurmond, whose family admits he was insane" (p. 245).

Alibi Five

The day after Jack Holmes had been arrested, sheriff's investigators learned that a lawyer for Holmes had obtained an alibi statement from a woman who placed Jack Holmes and his wife Evelyn with her and her husband on the evening when

Brooke Hart was kidnapped. Gertrude Estensen was interviewed by the undersheriff and a deputy:

> "Did you see Jack Holmes that Thursday, the ninth of November, the night Hart was kidnapped?"
>
> "Yes, that evening at my home."
>
> "Who was present?"
>
> "Mr. and Mrs. Holmes, my husband, and I."
>
> "Where did you go last Thursday evening, the night of the kidnapping?"
>
> "We went to the Hester Theater to see "*The Three Little Pigs*."
>
> "How do you fix the time?"
>
> "We were there before the end of the first show. They [Mr. and Mrs. Holmes], called my house shortly after dinner. We had done the dishes and were playing bridge when they walked in."
>
> "What time was that?"
>
> "Between 7:30 and 8:00; possibly a quarter to eight."
>
> "How do you fix the time that you went to the show?"
>
> "I know we had planned to go to the show one night that week, and we went Wednesday night. Then the Holmes came over unexpectedly, and we went to the show again on Thursday. We stayed at the house about fifteen or twenty minutes and then went to the Hester Theater."
>
> "Did Holmes tell you where he had been the night of the ninth?"

> "No."
>
> "Did he tell you he had been someplace and just got back?"
>
> "No, the Holmes' were not late when they came over, and he only remarked that his father and mother were at his house visiting, and that he had left them sitting there" (pp. 152, 153, 155, 156).

Swift Justice pondered some of the implications of Gertrude Estensen's recollections:

> "She [Estensen] had seriously impaired the credibility of both suspects' confessions. Could Holmes have intercepted Brooke Hart, taken him thirty-eight miles to the bridge, helped kill him, tossed him into the bay, returned to San Jose, picked up his wife, and driven to the Estensen home, all in a little more than ninety minutes? Possibly, perhaps with precision timing—but the crime had been dogged with delay at every step.
>
> "Holmes had forced Brooke Hart to drive out of the city by a roundabout route and then detour onto back country roads, and the stop-over to change the cars had been time-consuming. Then, after a false start to the bridge, the kidnappers had doubled back to recover Brooke's cigarettes.
>
> "At the killing site, it had taken more than a few minutes to bash in the victim's head, truss him up, and wire the concrete blocks to him. More time had elapsed while Thurmond descended to the bridge's underpinnings and fired a volley of bullets in Brooke's direction after he hit the water. There had been additional delays as the killers jettisoned their leftover block and wire, divided Brooke's ransom money, and composed the first ransom note.

> "All this before half past seven or eight o'clock? Hard to believe" (pp. 155-156).

Swift Justice also noted:

> "If Holmes had tarried at the bridge until anytime near 7:25 when the distress calls were heard, could he have really driven more than thirty miles back to San Jose, fetched Evelyn [his wife], and the Estensens, and arrived early for the nine o'clock show at the Hester Theater? [Sheriff], Emig declined to discuss time discrepancies when reporters quizzed him about them" (p. 160).

Sheriff Emig had a different take:

> "It was obvious, Emig insisted, that Holmes had set Gertrude up as an alibi witness and carried off his crime at breakneck speed to make the alibi work" (p. 158).

Corroborating Evidence

It is not uncommon for people arrested for the same crime to blame each other, or for interrogators to convince them to sign confessions with the false belief that they will not suffer the full consequences of the law since it wasn't their idea, or the other guy did most of the dirty work. Such confessions are not admissible in a court of law unless corroborated by independent facts.

Subsequent to the confessions, authorities found concrete blocks (one with blond hair stuck to it), wire, a hat with a BrookHart label (brand sold in L. Hart & Son's department store), and a pillowcase. The construction of the San Mateo Bridge, the longest bridge in the world at the time, had only been completed in 1929, so it would not be unusual for concrete and wire to litter the bottom of the bay.

The concrete block with hair stuck to it was provided to a physician at Agnews State Mental Hospital in Santa Clara County for examination, but no findings are on public record.

It turned out that the pillowcase allegedly used by the kidnappers to cover Brooke Hart's head, was the actor, Jackie Coogan's. A student at the University of Santa Clara, Coogan had attended a football game in Berkeley, and brought it with him in the car used to get to the game. It was stolen out of the car.

A deputy sheriff involved in the search conjectured:

> "Everything retrieved… might have been planted, and the cement blocks, the pieces of wire and the other exhibits placed where they were for purposes of confusion" (p. 164).

Marshall Hall, an attorney in the Oneal law firm, used his own boat to search for the body of Brooke Hart near the San Mateo Bridge:

> "I was always convinced, and I am now, that the bridge was a dumping place for bodies. There was another body there (besides Hart's), that we just didn't look into" (p. 159).

None of the corroborating evidence was ever used as the basis, together with the confessions, to indict Thurmond and Holmes for the kidnapping and murder of Brooke Hart.

Other Discrepancies

Thurmond Identifies Brooke Hart

Thurmond and Holmes would have both recognized Brooke Hart, particularly since he drove only one of only two 1933 Studebaker President roadsters in San Jose. Jack Holmes's father had custom tailored for L. Hart & Son for many years.

Holmes Wipes Off Fingerprints

For Jack Holmes to confess that he had wiped off fingerprints in the Studebaker (no prints of Thurmond or Holmes were found in Hart's car), and at the same time to confess to the use of his Chevrolet with his license plates to execute the kidnapping, drive to San Mateo Bridge, park it while Hart was killed, use it to make ransom calls from different pay phones in downtown San Jose, and park it in the same garage where Thurmond made the ransom call that resulted in his arrest, defies both credulity and the argument in *Swift Justice* about Jack Holmes's criminal expertise. The police searched Holmes's car, but did not find the either the gun or Brooke Hart's fingerprints.

Holmes Hits Hart on Head

Thurmond confessed that Holmes bashed Brooke Hart on the head twice with a twenty-two pound concrete block, while Holmes stated that he hit him with his fist. Thurmond confessed that Hart spoke and made noise after being struck in the head, but it would be highly unlikely for anyone to utter anything after they received two direct hits on the skull from such an impossibly heavy, coarse-edged object.

Murder Method

Holmes confessed that Thurmond tied the concrete blocks to Hart's feet before they threw him into the bay off the San Mateo Bridge, while Thurmond confessed that he only bound him hand and foot with clothesline wire.

Investigators found a witness at a concrete products company who stated that Thurmond purchased three twenty-two pound concrete blocks after he rejected blocks that were too light. If Thurmond intended to use concrete blocks to weigh Hart's body down, why did he confess that he had only trussed Brooke Hart's arms and feet with wire?

Kidnapping Plan

Thurmond and Holmes both confessed that they had discussed the crime only once or twice the day of or the day before the kidnapping, but the yard man at the concrete products company identified Thurmond as the man who purchased the concrete blocks on October 31st, ten days before the kidnapping.

Gun Purchase

A witness stated that Thurmond had purchased a gun from him in the middle of October, nearly a month prior to the kidnapping.

Unqualified Mastermind

Although *Swift Justice* portrayed Jack Holmes as the mastermind and Harold Thurmond as his foil, eyewitnesses for the purchase of the concrete blocks and a gun weeks before the crime imply that Thurmond was the "mastermind" of the Brooke Hart kidnapping.

Thurmond Climbed under the Bridge

Holmes confessed that Thurmond had climbed over the railing on one side of the bridge and shot at Brooke Hart while he turned the car around. When he returned, Thurmond climbed up over the railing on the other side of the bridge. It was virtually impossible—particularly at night—because of the design of the bridge underpinnings, to climb on the underside of the bridge from one side to the other. Thurmond made no such admission in his confession.

Ransom Meetings

Thurmond confessed that he and Holmes met five times following the kidnapping and murder: on Thursday November 9th , Friday November 10th , Saturday November 11th, Monday November 13th , Tuesday November 14th, and Wednesday November 15th.

Holmes confessed that Thurmond did not meet until Monday November 13th, and then again on November 14th and 15th. This discrepancy is important, because each time Thurmond and Holmes met after the kidnapping, Holmes allegedly provided Thurmond a separate ransom notes that Thurmond confessed to mailing.

Thurmond confessed that when they met on Friday November 10th, Holmes wrote a ransom demand on a post-card, and he borrowed his father's car and drove to Sacramento to mail it that night. Thurmond confessed he and Holmes met again on Saturday November 11th , when he received a second ransom note. On Monday November 13th , he mailed the second ransom note from San Francisco. Finally, Thurmond confessed that he received a third note from Holmes on November 15th, and mailed it from San Jose that morning.

Holmes confessed that he provided the first ransom note on Monday, November 13th, which Thurmond mailed from Sacramento that night. According to Holmes, he provided two additional ransom demands on November 14th and 15th, which Thurmond mailed, respectively, from San Francisco and San Jose.

The Wallet Toss

Thurmond confessed that he and Holmes had agreed to toss, for a never explained reason, Hart's wallet into the San Francisco Bay. Thurmond also confessed that Holmes specifically instructed him to take the ferry to Oakland, and toss the wallet from the ferry. Holmes confessed to nothing about the wallet. The guardrail was underwater when Thurmond confessed he tossed it.

Thurmond's Failed Ransom Call

Thurmond confessed that his first attempt (at 9:30 p.m.) to make a ransom call to the Hart mansion failed. Brooke's sister Aleese provided a verbatim account of the conversation with a man who claimed to have Brooke at 9:30 p.m. on the night he disappeared.

"Some Woman"

Thurmond confessed that when he had made the second ransom call he spoke to "some woman." This evidenced that he did not know with whom he had spoken. The verbatim record of the conversation between the kidnapper and Miriam Hart evidenced that the caller addressed her by name.

Sacramento Postmark on Ransom Demand

Thurmond confessed that he borrowed his father's Pontiac and drove to Sacramento on Friday night, November 10th. Holmes confessed that Thurmond mailed the ransom demand from Sacramento on Monday, November 13th.

Thurmond Gets Second Ransom Note

Thurmond confessed that he received the second ransom note from Holmes on Saturday November 11th, while Holmes confessed that he provided it to Thurmond on Tuesday, November 14th.

Holmes outside Garage

Holmes confessed that he had waited in his car outside the garage where Thurmond was arrested. Thurmond did not confess that Holmes was with him.

Part IV Mastermind and Foil

Swift Justice's establishment of the argument for the "long-accepted" version of the kidnap and murder facts required the formulation of the criminal motivation and means for two men who "had never been in trouble before in their lives" (p. x), to kidnap and murder Brooke Hart.

Swift Justice offers some tortured reasons why, out of the blue, Thurmond and Holmes committed a brazen kidnapping in a town where they would be recognized by a large number of people. To establish the rationale to explain their sudden, brutal criminality, *Swift Justice* relied on eccentric personal memories for which there is no test for veracity, information from family, acquaintances, members of law enforcement, and a surfeit of artistic license.

Swift Justice's tracking of Jack Holmes's emergent criminal nature started with Holmes in high school. His biology teacher, "a humorless disciplinarian," became annoyed by Holmes's wisecracks, and the "outbursts of giggling" (p. 81), they caused, and ordered everyone to take the final examination.

Holmes made another comment, and the teacher announced that he was "flunking you right now" (p. 83). When the teacher discovered that Holmes had drawn a "devastating cartoon of . . . the teacher's. . . face on the head of a jackass" (p. 81), he sent Holmes to the principal's office, where he was "expelled . . . on the spot" (p. 81).

There have been, and remain, tens of thousands, if not hundreds of thousands, of teenage boys who run afoul of teachers and principals, but such behavior is not the precursor or predictor of whether they will commit a capital crime. In strange contradiction to this trifling example of Holmes's nascent criminality, *Swift Justice* also documented examples of his many positive traits:

> "Holmes was . . . a self-taught pianist; he could play anything by ear. Most of the time he was quietly courteous and personable. Most people thought him handsome, . . . with his ample pompadour rising above magnetic blue eyes. A cleft chin and a hint of cruelty in his down-turned mouth line only heightened his magnetism" (p. 82).

At twenty, Jack Holmes wed Evelyn Fleming: "He had all the personality in the world. He was everything I ever dreamed of having" (p. 83). A year after he married, Holmes became a salesman for the Standard Oil Company (p. 83). Holmes's wedding:

> "Commenced a nine year period of domesticity when, to all appearances, Holmes was close to a model husband and good father" (p. 83).

Jack Holmes seemed to impress people even on first contact, and over time obtained the respect that would admit him to important civic and social memberships with the leaders of the community in which he lived:

> "Theron Fox, then the sports editor of the *Mercury Herald*, was impressed when Jack appeared in the newsroom to hand-deliver his first credit card. "He was the type of guy that if your sister or daughter brought him home, you'd say, 'He's a great catch, the All-American boy.' Not only was Holmes industrious, he

> sought community respect. In 1926, following his father's footsteps, he became a Mason, joining Golden Rule Lodge 479" (p. 83).

Focused on isolated anecdotal evidence of Holmes's nascent criminality, *Swift Justice* did identify one soul who asserted Holmes's "engaging personality camouflaged a mean temper and a streak of ruthless rebellion" (p. 83). The man had sold a car to Holmes and when payments were missed, he had tried to repossess it.

Holmes appeared with a three-foot length of axle, and threatened him. Based on this isolated event, the man believed that Holmes was "just a natural criminal" (p. 84).

Swift Justice documented considerable evidence of the positive aspects of Holmes's character, but underscored isolated examples of the negative over the overwhelmingly positive to establish the motivation for the kidnapping and murder of Brooke Hart.

By twenty-three, now the father of a boy and a girl, Holmes had been transferred by Standard Oil to Half Moon Bay where he lived for two or three years (p. 84). According to *Swift Justice*:

> "The gas station out of which Holmes worked became a hangout for Prohibition runners and bootleggers and for highjackers ashore. Holmes soaked up their scofflaw braggadocio. Their contempt for the laws they broke and the cops they bribed touched his resonant chord of greed" (p. 84).

Swift Justice did not identify the source of information about the criminals where Holmes had worked, or the inflammatory assertion that Holmes was not only a sponge who soaked up their criminality, but possessed a "resonant chord of greed" that they had plucked.

Swift Justice's only other alledgedly ominous evidence about Jack Holmes's emergent criminal pathology was approximated at the time of his enrollment at San Jose Teachers' College (now San Jose State University). Apparently, Holmes's emergent criminality was restricted only to educational institutions:

> "He took a battery of entrance examinations, including an intelligence test in which he scored well, and an 'A and S' (ascendency and submissiveness) test to discern leadership potential. He scored 'plus-13,' placing in the upper fifth of the test group" (pp. 84-85).

If Holmes had not been arrested and lynched, such test results boded well for his future. In *Swift Justice,* the sole application of his intelligence and leadership potential was to mastermind the lamest kidnapping in American history. *Swift Justice* contains an unattributed anecdote to support the case for Holmes's hidden hard-core criminality:

> "It was during this time that his fellow students noticed his "perfect crime" fixation. He would pore over newspapers, analyzing the crimes reported and the errors that led to the perpetrators' detection. One friend considered him 'almost devilishly clever about it'" (p. 85).

The *Swift Justice* characterization of Holmes as a criminal mastermind demanded that he be provided a foil to carry out the dirty work:

> "Jack Holmes…need[ed]…someone he could dominate. No one could have better filled the role than Thomas Harold Thurmond, for whom submissiveness was a way of life" (p. 85).

Thurmond's submissive nature arose at the hands of his mother and sisters:

> "Thurmond had grown up as a plodding younger son in a devoutly Baptist home dominated by his mother and five sisters" (p. 85). Lillie Thurmond, Harold's mother; "was a matriarchal personage, a pillar of the church" (p. 86).

> "Under her roof no meal was begun until grace was said. To her, liquor was Satan's brew, and she militantly guarded her daughters and boarders against its corruption" (p. 86).

The only mention about Thurmond's father is about his sale of a service station where one of the conditions was that the purchaser had to hire his son (p. 86).

> "That transaction is one of the few clear views we have of his father…a Kentuckian by birth who remains in the shadows of history" (p. 86).

The sheriff, the FBI, or even the press should have verified whether Thurmond's father permitted his son to borrow his car repeatedly day and night during the six days between the kidnapping and his arrest. There appears no documentation in *Swift Justice,* FBI files, or in newspaper accounts that Thurmond's father was asked, or provided an answer to this operative question.

Harold Thurmond's family had expressed deep worries about his mental state:

> "Lillie Thurmond regarded her son Harold as a 'delicate' lad, especially after he suffered a severe head injury in early childhood" (p. 87).

> "Later…we observed indications of considerable mental dullness" (p. 246).

> "The family had considered placing him [Harold] in an

> asylum. They were convinced that he entirely became deranged and reason had completely left him" (p. 246).

Swift Justice summarized the prevalent social perception of Harold Thurmond:

> "As he grew into manhood it became increasingly evident to most that Harold was a dullard in a family of high achievers" (p. 87).

The man who provided Thurmond a job when he bought a service station from his father noted:

> "I wouldn't classify him as retarded exactly, but he was just not very smart. I guess he had about an eight year old mentality. He was very easily led" (p. 87).

Thurmond dropped out of high school, worked as a yard-man at a lumber company, then at a paint store in Oakland. When he returned to San Jose, he worked a day or two at a time until his father arranged the job at the service station (p. 87). Since Holmes was a gasoline and oil salesman who called upon service station owners, they had allegedly met at the service station where Harold Thurmond worked.

The Kidnapping Plan

Thurmond and Holmes both confessed that they had discussed the kidnapping only once or twice the day of or the day before they had committed it. This haphazard plan, as conventional wisdom had it, was the reason why the kidnapping was star-crossed. It was the senseless actions of two greedy fast-buck artists who committed murder solely to get the money they needed to satisfy the material needs of the women they loved; just another good reason to lynch them.

Swift Justice identified Jack Holmes as both the self-trained criminal mastermind whose felonious brain came up with the plan to kidnap Brooke Hart, and the brash ignoramus whose kidnapping scheme and implementation was arguably the worst in recorded history. Thurmond's and Holmes's confessions painted a different picture.

A comparison of the confessions reveals that it was primarily Thurmond (the man who would "happily stick his head in an oven if anyone asked him to") who not only, as Holmes had confessed, wanted to kidnap Brooke Hart, but also wanted to "dump him." Witnesses identified Thurmond as the man who bought concrete blocks and a gun three weeks before the kidnapping.

Given Thurmond's and Holmes's lifestyles, the murder of Brooke Hart shortly after he was abducted was the only way they could have carried out the kidnapping. In the court of public opinion, these unremarkable lifestyles helped convict them.

At the time of the kidnapping, Holmes lived with his wife, two children, and his mother-in-law in a neighborhood a few miles from downtown San Jose; Thurmond with his parents.

Mastermind

Swift Justice's criminal mastermind, Jack Holmes, devised and implemented an astonishingly incompetent kidnap and murder plan:

- Holmes, a married salesman with two children, selected as his partner in crime, a brain damaged dim-wit without a car that still lived, at twenty-eight-years-of-age, with his mother and father.

- Holmes had discussed the kidnapping with dim-wit Thurmond only once or twice.

- At 5:00 p.m. on the night of the kidnapping, Holmes visited a friend who lived on the southern city limits of San Jose, and remained with her until just before 6:00 p.m.

- At 6:00 p.m., parked in Holmes's Chevrolet with his license plates near one of the busiest intersections of the town in which they had both grown up and could be recognized, Holmes and Thurmond waited for Brooke Hart to exit the L. Hart & Son parking lot.

- On the sidewalk outside the department store on a well-lit, busy street filled with home-bound pedestrians and cars, the well-known Holmes climbed on the running board of Brooke's Studebaker, and entered to stick a gun in his ribs.

- Holmes ordered Thurmond to drive his Chevrolet and to meet him in Milpitas.

- Holmes forced Brooke Hart to drive his Studebaker on a zigzag course through the middle of San Jose to a point on Evans Road in Milpitas some seven miles east of San Jose. Thurmond met him in Holmes's Chevrolet just before 7:00 p.m. Holmes wiped the interior of the Studebaker for fingerprints.

- With Hart held at gunpoint by Thurmond in the back seat of his two-door Chevrolet, Holmes drove toward the San Mateo Bridge, drove back to the Studebaker to get his cigarettes, then drove to the San Mateo Bridge. He had to pay a toll based on the number of occupants in his vehicle before he entered the seven mile long private span.

- Holmes parked his car either one half or three and one half miles from the eastern entrance, ordered Hart from the car, and either hit him on the head with a concrete block or his fist. Thurmond bound Hart's arms and legs with wire, and either did or did not tie the concrete blocks to his feet.

- Holmes ordered Thurmond to crawl under the bridge, shoot at Hart, then climb up the railing on the opposite side.

- Holmes ordered Thurmond to throw Hart's wallet into the San Francisco Bay and not keep anything that could prove they were the kidnappers.

- Before he ordered Thurmond to borrow his father's car (on a bridge only eighteen miles from San Francisco) and drive to San Francisco, make ransom calls, throw Hart's wallet into the bay without removing the identification, and then drive sixty miles back home, Holmes drove over forty miles back to San Jose.

- Back in downtown San Jose from the San Mateo Bridge, Holmes took time to write a ransom note for Thurmond to mail in Sacramento. He then raced to pick up his wife and then to the home of friends. Based on the documented statements of five witnesses, he arrived on time.

- Although Holmes had just been on a wind-swept bridge high above the San Francisco Bay, supposedly hit Brooke Hart on the head twice with a twenty-two pound concrete block that probably caused blood to fly, trussed him with wire and tossed him into the bay, then raced home in a lather, his wife Evelyn, mother Hulda Holmes, and Gertrude Estensen stated that Holmes looked and acted normal.

- Gertrude Estensen stated that on the night of the kidnapping and murder Holmes and his wife arrived at her home between 7:30 and 7:45 p.m., Thurmond and Holmes both had confessed that they had arrived in downtown San Jose just before 8:00 p.m.

- Holmes ordered Thurmond to borrow his father's car to drive to San Francisco, make the ransom calls, and throw Brooke Hart's wallet into the bay. At 9:30 p.m. at a speakeasy on Market Street in San Francisco, Thurmond used a telephone on the bar to call the Hart home. He confessed he was unable to complete the call.

- At 10:30 p.m. on a hotel pay phone, Thurmond told "some woman" that he wanted $40,000 for Brooke. Miriam Hart stated that the caller had addressed her by name.

- Thurmond walked to Pier 32 and had tossed Brooke Hart's wallet into San Francisco Bay. Thurmond then drove some sixty miles to San Jose to arrive by midnight.

- Holmes stated that he didn't meet with Thurmond until Monday November 13th. Thurmond stated that they met on Friday November 11th, the day after the kidnapping; Saturday November 12th, then Monday, Tuesday, and Wednesday of the following week.

- Holmes wrote the ransom notes, and ordered Thurmond to borrow his father's car to mail them from Sacramento and San Francisco.

- Holmes specified the following of Alex Hart in the first ransom demand: (1) get $40,000 in unmarked bills of different denominations and put in black satchel; (2)

take a week's trip in the Studebaker on an hour's notice; (3) install a radio in Brooke's Studebaker (which already had a radio), and (4) await further ransom instructions that would be broadcast on NBC radio station KPO. Holmes, a lifelong resident of San Jose whose father did custom tailor work for L. Hart & Son, ignored the fact that Alex Hart had never learned to drive.

- Holmes ordered dim-wit Thurmond to be the telephone ransom negotiator who had to think on his feet when challenged by the highly intelligent and world-wise father of the kidnap victim.
- Holmes ordered Thurmond to make ransom calls to the Hart home from pay phones in downtown San Jose during an intense police dragnet.
- Holmes continued to ignore the well-known fact that Alex Hart didn't drive, and ordered him, in the second ransom note, to place the money in a satchel, and keep it in Brooke's Studebaker as he drove to where he would be ordered to go on a moment's notice.
- From a tapped pay phone in downtown San Jose, Thurmond ordered Alex Hart to take the night train to Los Angeles.
- Holmes wrote a third ransom note that again ordered Alex Hart to drive the Studebaker with the money, this time, to Los Angeles at ten miles per hour.
- The night after the third ransom note had been received, Holmes tried, but aborted two calls to the Hart mansion from pay phones eight blocks away from each other in downtown San Jose. Holmes drove between pay phones in his car with his license plates.

- Holmes ordered Thurmond to use the pay phone in the same garage where he had parked his car since he moved into the California Hotel three days earlier after he had separated from his wife. The garage was 150 feet from San Jose Police headquarters. Holmes waited for Thurmond in his Chevrolet outside the garage.
- Holmes failed to notice sheriff's deputies, police, and FBI agents rush into the garage, and went for a drive.
- A hour later, Holmes parked his car in the same garage, had dinner at a nearby tavern, and went to bed. The garage attendant stated Holmes wore a light blue suit and a panama hat, and was in good spirits. He never looked for Thurmond.

Holmes's Motivation

At the time of the kidnapping, Jack Holmes had established a successful career as an oil and gas salesman. While craven greed was the catch-all for the kidnapping and murder of Brooke Hart, Holmes lived, compared to most of his friends and neighbors, a very comfortable life:

> "Above all, Holmes was gainfully employed, which in itself was no mean status symbol in . . . 1933. In May, riding high, he traded his battered old Chevrolet on a handsome new model, a black 1933 Chevy coach (p. 88).

Holmes had lost his job with an oil company after the kidnapping, but was being recruited to sell gas and oil directly to agricultural businesses:

> "It became clear that whatever compelled Holmes to kidnapping, murder, and extortion, it was not abject poverty. Unlike many jobless in 1933, he was not 'up against it.' His unemployment was only in passing; within his grasp was a position that might pay $100-200 a week—several times what families were living on in comfort" (p. 149).

Despite his relative financial success compared to other San Jose residents at the height of the Great Depression, according to *Swift Justice,* it was Holmes's greed coupled with his unrequited love for a woman that made him kidnap and murder Brooke Hart.

Holmes's Siren was a former high school sweetheart he had contacted years after each of their marriages. As the result of the reunion, Holmes and his wife, and the former sweetheart and her husband began to socialize together on a regular basis (including the night of the kidnapping and murder).

Holmes's romantic interest in the woman had caused him and his wife to separate three days before he was arrested. *Swift Justice* elevates a not unknown occurrence among married adults to pathological evidence of Holmes's criminality:

> "The fantasy of making love to her besieged Jack's troubled mind. He came to realize that possessing Gertrude, whether as wife, mistress, or playmate, would require far more money than he would ever make selling gasoline and oil" (p. 89).

Santa Clara County Deputy Sheriff Howard Buffington interviewed the woman and attempted to flesh out the suspicion that she was the cause of Holmes's avarice.

> "Did he talk about having money?"

"He never mentioned money. We were not that friendly that we discussed money matters."

"Did he at any time say that he expected to get some money in a couple of weeks?"

"No, he always seemed to have plenty of money when we were out together, the four of us, but never any superfluous amount."

"When he wanted you to go away with him, didn't he discuss how he was going to get the money?"

"No. There was no intention on my part of running away with him, so I would not be interested in money matters. If I were interested in the idea, naturally I would have such a discussion…I possibly could have found out if I inquired, but I did not."

"You cannot think of any time when there was anything said about the money?"

"No."

"Who paid for the tickets for the show last Thursday night?"

"My husband paid for mine, and Mr. Holmes paid for his wife. We always did that" (pp. 152, 153, 154).

Holmes's love interest not only lived with her husband, but her mother and father. In most instances when he was with her, her husband, mother, father, or Holmes's wife Evelyn were present. While Holmes may have had a romantic interest in this woman, she had not succumbed to his attentions, and money was not an issue.

Holmes's Means

Judged by his performance as a "crime expert" in the kidnap and murder of Brooke Hart, Jack Holmes had internalized only those criminal methods guaranteed to result in his arrest. He had no place to keep or watch over a kidnap victim, and he also was expected to both work, and play a daily role in his wife's and both of his children's lives.

While the "long-accepted" version of the guilt of Jack Holmes had him commit a kidnapping and murder the same night he was with his wife and friends, he had to accomplish such acts over geographical distances for which there is a specific measure of time.

According to the analysis in *Swift Justice*, Jack Holmes could not have driven the distances within the time frame identified in his confession. In addition, even the most ignorant criminal would not use their own car (with identifying license plates) in the commission of the crime, particularly if he was widely known and readily recognized member of the community. *Swift Justice* documented the intimacy shared by the citizens of San Jose in its description of the three families most directly affected by the kidnapping:

> "Virtually everyone in the city…knew the Hart's, the Holmes's, or the Thurmond's, or all three…." (p. x).

The lives of most people in San Jose, one way or another, were intertwined with L. Hart & Son. Hart's, in its many incarnations, had been located at the corner of Market and Santa Clara Streets since its founding in 1866 by Alex Hart's father, Leopold Hart (p. 24).

> "In San Jose Hart's store was more of an institution than the city hall. It was a gathering place and a club. On 'Dollar Days' people swarmed there for bargains

> like women's and misses; knit dresses for one dollar, overalls for fifty-nine cents, work shirts for fifty cents, men's two-trouser suits for $24.95, coal and wood ranges for $59.50, two-piece chesterfield sets for $24.95, playing cards for nineteen cents a deck, and Lifebuoy soap at five cakes for twenty-nine cents" (p. 24).
>
> "Thousands of San Joseans knew Brooke Hart. Housewives saw him two or three times a week when they shopped. They had watched him grow up" (p. 24).

Thurmond's Motivation

Thurmond was engaged, but the woman broke it off two years before the kidnapping:

> "Thurmond said he had been in love once, but the girl turned him down, and married another" (p. 115).
>
> "An invitation to her wedding to a rival suitor, which Harold found in his mail…, demolished his last remnant of self-esteem. Plunging into depression, he began to drink, taking up with a lawless crowd . . . ." (p. 87).
>
> "He had not seen her again until that very afternoon [day of kidnapping], when he had caught a glimpse of her and gone to pieces" (p. 115).

Ipso facto, Holmes and Thurmond were kindred spirits. In the court of public opinion, it was accepted as a perfectly sane reason for their utterly insane foray into capital kidnapping and murder:

> "Thurmond, whose own poverty had cost him a woman's love, was a sympathetic listener to Holmes's woes" (p. 89).

In addition to having fallen to pieces over the loss of the love of his life, Thurmond was a submissive who was easy prey to the more powerful Jack Holmes. Thurmond was also compliant in his relationship with his family:

> "Harold attended church out of habit.... If his mother wanted him in the pew, he was there—because he always acquiesced to the wishes of a stronger personality" (pp. 87-88).

Swift Justice imagined Holmes's rationale for selecting this dullard as his partner in crime:

> "[Holmes] would need a partner who would follow his orders blindly—someone with a ruthless streak, not overly sensitive to the distance between rights and wrong, nonetheless reliable" (pp. 90-91).

Thomas Harold Thurmond, reliable? Holmes apparently didn't worry that his fellow kidnapper and murderer would have to ask his father to borrow the car each time he needed a kidnapping task completed, or that a uniformly perceived dim-wit could handle ransom negotiations with the strong-willed Alex Hart. Holmes didn't check in with Thurmond until four days after the kidnapping, and evidenced, as the ransom negotiations progressed, no interest in the outcomes of the tasks he had ordered him to complete.

Thurmond's Means

Thomas Harold Thurmond had no independent means to carry out the extortion tasks Holmes had assigned to him. A dullard whose maturity was arrested in childhood, Thurmond would be the least likely person in the world to negotiate ransom with anyone, much less Alex Hart. Although the Hart family identified the "calm, well-modulated" voice of the kidnapper as being Thurmond's, it is virtually impossible that he could have carried out such a stressful and crucial role according to the interaction documented in the record of the ransom negotiations.

Thurmond lived with his mother, father, sisters, and paying boarders. Thurmond had supposedly borrowed his father's car repeatedly, and returned it all hours of the day and night. Given that his fundamentalist Baptist, tee-totaling mother kept a gimlet eye on all that went on in her home, consecutive requests for use of the family car would have generated sharp questions. Thurmond simply could not have avoided the scrutiny of his mother, or provided an acceptable rationale for the use of the family car day after day and night after night.

It was also noted in *Swift Justice* that the Thurmond family had to let rooms in their home to make ends meet, so the family car would be viewed as a precious resource. No evidence corroborated its use in the Brooke Hart kidnapping.

Criminal Propensities

The precursor to Thurmond's Olympic leap into kidnapping, murder, and extortion was being fired from a service station because of the disappearance of cash and gasoline. The service station owner met with both Harold and his father. Although he did not confess, Harold signed (and his father co-signed), a promissory note to guarantee the repayment of the amount of the cash and gasoline that had disappeared during Harold's shifts (p. 89).

Although Thurmond and Holmes only had a kidnapping complaint filed against them by Sheriff Emig, *Swift Justice* identified armed robberies to which Thurmond, between his arrest and his lynching, had allegedly confessed to Sheriff Emig. Another man had been previously arrested for the crimes after being identified by a witness.

As training for the Brooke Hart kidnapping and murder, according to *Swift Justice,* Holmes supposedly ordered Harold Thurmond to rob, in Holmes's car with his license plates, oil companies at which he had been employed over the previous eight years.

Holmes identified the Union Oil Company employee who was responsible for depositing the day's receipts:

> "As [the Union Oil employee] slowed for a turn…, Thurmond [in Holmes's car], ran him to the curb and entered his car at gunpoint. Thurmond was steady on the trigger, his face blank, and his manner devoid of emotion" (p. 91).

The depiction of Thurmond as "steady on the trigger*,"* was in vivid contradiction to the description provided by a man who subsequently claimed he sold Thurmond the handgun that was supposed to have been used in the kidnapping and murder of Brooke Hart:

> "[Thurmond] From the awkward way he handled it, [the witness], concluded that he had little experience with firearms" (pp. 92-93).

If Thurmond already possessed the gun he used in the armed robbery of the oil company receipts, and appeared to brandish it with great facility, why would he subsequently purchase another gun and appear like he had never touched one before?

Would Jack Holmes, whose entire career was spent employed at major oil companies in San Jose, order a dim-wit accomplice to use his identifiable car in the armed robberies of individuals he knew personally?

Thurmond's limited mental capacity and subservient nature demonstrably facilitated his ready admission to any crime of which he was accused, whether it be the kidnapping and murder of Brooke Hart, or armed robbery.

In the context of Harold Thurmond's larcenous behavior, *Swift Justice* imagined Jack Holmes's deliberative process as his nascent criminal mentality manifested:

> "An egoist…, Holmes convinced himself that he was smarter than those [kidnappers], who had been caught. In that frame of mind he must have noticed, in the September 19 *Mercury Herald*, the overwritten account of the gala Hart's Department Store dinner at the DeAnza [hotel], the night before. The headline read:
>
> "BROOKE L. HART MADE EXECUTIVE IN HIS FATHER'S FIRM" (p. 90).

Swift Justice guessed Holmes's fevered reaction to the headline:

> "Slowly a plan for self-enrichment began to germinate in Holmes's fertile, criminally attuned, sexually haunted mind. He would have to work it in easy stages, and he would need a partner who would follow orders blindly" (p. 90).

The dim bulb in Jack Holmes's criminal mastermind flubbed on: Thomas Harold Thurmond.

Part V The Lynching

The reaction of the people of San Jose to the atrocities confessed by Thurmond and Holmes was unambiguous at all levels of society:

> "Since the day of Brooke Hart's disappearance, a surly, swollen tide of unrest had risen. It saturated the establishment circles in which the Hart family moved, the bully-boy rednecks of the street, the youthful thrill-seekers, and the desperate ranks of the idle jobless. The First Street businessmen were as much a part of it as Brooke's stalwart friends at Santa Clara University" (p. 127).

Sheriff Emig learned of the threats to the lives of Thurmond and Holmes right after their arrests and decided to get them out of San Jose "before the courthouse opened for the day" (p. 128). Emig dressed Thurmond and Holmes in mechanic's uniforms borrowed from a garage owner near the jail, and took them to the Potrero Hill police station in San Francisco.

While Thurmond and Holmes remained in jail in San Francisco, extensive efforts were underway to locate the body of Brooke Hart. In addition to boats manned by law enforcement personnel, citizens also dragged the bay in private watercraft. Airplanes and a Navy blimp were used in an attempt to spot a body; even a dummy was dropped off the bridge into the water to determine how the tides and current would carry it. None of the efforts produced the desired result. The *San Francisco Chronicle* summarized the failure to find the corpus delecti:

> "It is generally admitted that the murder angle of the case depends upon finding the body of young Hart" (p. 169).

Without Brooke Hart's corpse, and after he had waited and waited for the district attorney of Santa Clara County to indict the two men for kidnapping and murder, United States Attorney H.H. McPike convinced a federal grand jury in San Francisco to indict Thurmond and Holmes for mail fraud. It was the only federal law that the accused kidnappers had violated:

> "The federal indictment specified…three counts of using the mails to obtain ransom, three of using the mails to threaten bodily harm, and one of conspiracy 'with other persons unknown.' The charges carried a maximum punishment of 122 years in prison and a $40,000 fine for each kidnapper. Bail was fixed at $50,000." (p. 180).

McPike sent U.S. marshals to take the two suspects into custody in San Francisco, but the San Francisco police would only release Thurmond and Holmes to the Santa Clara County sheriff. Sheriff Emig immediately returned Thurmond and Holmes to San Jose. The lynching took place four days later.

If McPike had not obtained an indictment and sent U.S. marshals to arrest Thurmond and Holmes in the week before the body was found in San Francisco Bay, they would still have been in the San Francisco city jail sixty some miles the night they were lynched.

Huge battering ram being used by Holmes-Thurmond lynchers on San Jose jail – *Courtesy of the Bancroft Library, University of California, Berkeley*

The Santa Clara County grand jury never issued an indictment against Thurmond and Holmes, rather Sheriff Emig signed a “complaint” that accused them solely of the kidnapping, but not the murder of Brooke Hart.

> “They [Holmes and Thurmond] willfully, unlawfully, and feloniously seize, abduct, conceal, and kidnap and carry away an individual, to wit, Brooke Hart, and thereby commit extortion and exact from friends and relatives of Brooke Hart money and other valuable things [sic]” (p. 180).

Upon rumors of insanity pleas, two psychiatrists from Agnews State Mental Hospital in Santa Clara County interviewed both Thurmond and Holmes. Following a half an hour interview with Harold Thurmond, one psychiatrist answered the operative question as to whether Thurmond was crazy:

> “No, his responses to my questions were prompt and lucid. They were those of an entirely normal person. He struck me as a man almost sick with fear and remorse, but sane” (p. 188).

A second psychiatrist, an “alienist,” interviewed both Thurmond and Holmes and concluded that they were both perfectly normal. He reported:

> “Holmes was the more intelligent of the two. His motive was clearly for the money… . Thurmond had no motive; he was merely the tool of Holmes’s intellect” (p. 189).

On the Friday before the lynching, the announcement was issued that the search for Brooke Hart’s body was being abandoned. San Mateo County Sheriff J. J. McGrath:

> "We are convinced that the body of Brooke Hart is not near the bridge. It appears now that he struggled free of at least one of the weights fastened to him, and perhaps from the second one also. If this is true his body probably floated away from the bridge and may now be anywhere in the bay" (p. 189).

On November 18, 1933, a stunning front-page story appeared in the *Oakland Tribune* headlined: "Conflicting Stories by Kidnappers Raise Doubt":

> "Even the confessed slayers of the boy [Brooke Hart], do not know where it is for they were the tools of 'higher-ups' who took charge of Hart after he was kidnapped.
>
> "This is the startling belief held today by members of the Alexander Hart family according to spokesman and intimate friend of the family who has been with them since the boy disappeared. Several officials investigating the crime agreed with the family of the millionaire merchant in their beliefs.
>
> "The things that Thomas Thurmond and John Holmes claim to have done are physically impossible, said the spokesman for the family.
>
> "For example, Thurmond is supposed to have climbed out on a stringer of the bridge, fired shots at Brooke, and then climbed under the bridge to come up on the other side. We know this to be impossible because of the bridge construction.
>
> "The Hart family, while convinced that Brooke was cruelly murdered, is firm in the belief that the murder did not take place where the two men say it did, …
>
> "They believe that Thurmond and Holmes committed

> the actual kidnapping, but turned their victim to others who killed the youth and disposed of the body."

The story appeared three days after the arrests and confessions of Thurmond and Holmes when, after a comprehensive search of the bay, the body of Brooke Hart was not found. Despite the shocking opinions of the Hart family, no other newspaper included them in their coverage.

The day prior to the lynching, Royce Brier, the *San Francisco Chronicle* reporter who won a Pulitzer Prize for his coverage of the Brooke Hart kidnapping, had an article published about the "old time vigilante committee," that had formed in San Jose. Even the organizers of the San Jose vigilance committee realized that the confessions alone, even with the alleged corroborating evidence found in the bay, would not justify a lynching:

> "It is understood that no action will be taken by the committee,…unless and until the body of the slain youth is recovered. This precaution leader's [sic] feel is absolutely necessary before any action by the committee could be justified in the eyes of the public" (p. 190).

But word was out on the street:

> "They had the word out—a bunch of businessmen downtown, the [Sheriff] Emig gang, the politicians. It was rolling, rolling, rolling" (p. 191).
>
> "It was all over the street that they were going to lynch those guys. You know, the storekeepers would tell their employees. It was just like a loudspeaker going over" (p. 191).

Maurice Holmes, Jack Holmes's father, hired attorney Vincent Hallinan in San Francisco:

> "Maurice produced a packet of small bills totaling $10,000—a stupendous sum for a man of ordinary means to have scraped together in 1933" (p. 193).

Hallinan called Governor Rolph:

> "I have been retained to represent Jack Holmes in San Jose. As you know, there is a lynching threat down there, and if there is violence, I want my client protected. We may need the militia."
>
> "If they lynch those fellows, I'll pardon the lynchers."
>
> "Well, that's a hell of a thing for the governor of the state to say; you're supposed to enforce the laws!" (p. 193).

Later, reporters caught up with Governor Rolph in Los Angeles:

> "I'm not going to call out the Guard to protect the kidnappers who willfully killed that fine boy" (p. 193).

Despite the relentless march toward the enforcement of lynch law against Thurmond and Holmes for the kidnap and murder of Brooke Hart, the Hart family remained the recipient of communications from people who claimed to have their son:

> "Now, ten days after the Thurmond and Holmes confessions, two new ransom notes turned up in the Hart's mail, insisting that Brooke still lived. Three similar telephone calls, offering to return him for ransom, were taken.... The FBI, which had withdrawn its agents to San Francisco after the arrests, reactivated the investigation on the million-to-one chance that one of the new offers could be legitimate" (p. 194).

At 5:00 a.m. on Sunday, November 26th, two duck hunters in a boat one half mile south of the San Mateo Bridge, felt a soft thud:

> "My God, it's a man!" (p. 195).

The body was terribly decomposed:

> "Crabs and fish had fed upon it, and from the waist up it was hardly more than a skeleton. Much of the skull was exposed, as was the rib cage. The left lung was mostly intact, but the other organs of the chest cavity and the abdomen were missing. The face and hair were eaten away. The arm bones were still in the shoulder sockets, but the hands were gone. The corpse was coatless, and there were only remnants of a shirt, but trousers still clothed the lower part. The feet were in bad shape, but socks and garters remained" (p. 196).

About 10:00 a.m., Sheriff Emig received a call about the body from his counterpart in Alameda County where it had been discovered. Instantly, the word spread:

> "In the next ten minutes, from telephones in or near Emig's office, calls went out along the wires to certain recipients throughout Santa Clara County and beyond. In an inexorable chain reaction, the recipients called others. By 10:15, scores were aware of the discovery of Brooke Hart's wretched remains—the action signal for the vigilantes. By 10:30, hundreds knew; by 10:45, thousands" (p. 198).

The news media, primed for the discovery of a body, were on the story immediately:

> "(*S.F. Chronicle*) The paper's city desk alerted five other staffers remaining on duty in San Jose, who immediately called their well-placed sources on the

> vigilance committee. Meanwhile, the pressmen, stereotypers, engravers, Linotype operators, carriers, and newsboys were called in. To the *Chronicle* editors, . . . the lynching was not just something that might happen; it was going to happen" (p. 199).

On the eastern shore of the San Francisco Bay south of the San Mateo Bridge, Sheriff Emig arrived with Hart employees who identified the shirt, pants, socks, and garters on the body as coming from the store. Brooke Hart's dentist checked the teeth of the corpse against his dental records and determined that they matched (p. 200). Subsequently, autopsy surgeons examined the corpse:

> "Besides the indentation at the rear of the skull, they found a fracture of the right temple, and a wound on the top of the head. Any one of the three injuries might have caused death. The decomposed legs bore lesions that might have been bullet holes, but X-rays found no bullets in the corpse" (p. 201).

> "The autopsy told [Sheriff] Emig that both killers . . . were . . . lying about how their victim was killed. Jack Holmes had not hit Brooke over the head with a brick like Thurmond said; nor had the boy's head struck the concrete of the bridge like Holmes said. The skull fractures were characteristic of injuries left by the butt of a revolver. Brooke had been pistol whipped, by which kidnapper it was impossible to tell" (p. 201).

Citizens contacted Bay Area newspapers to confirm the reports that the body of Brooke Hart had been found, and that the lynching would take place that night. The publisher of the *San Jose News* took advantage of the event:

> "[The] Publisher. . . mobilized virtually his whole staff to crank out two extras, although the paper did not normally publish on Sunday. They were bastardized editions with only the front pages bearing Sunday datelines; the Saturday plates were left on the rest of the pages. It mattered not; 12,000 papers were sold right in town…." (p. 199).

On their drive back from Alameda County where he had helped identify the body of Brooke Hart, L. Hart & Son manager Louis Rossi warned Sheriff Emig of what the vigilantes had planned:

> "They are going to break into your building tonight, and they're going to capture the kidnappers, and they're going to hang them across the street in St. James Park. Have those deputies guarding those prisoners put their guns away to avoid bloodshed" (p. 201).

FBI Special Agent in Charge Vetterli, also in the car, affirmed Rossi's advisement:

> "Bill, you listen to Louie Rossi, he knows what he is talking about" (pp. 201-202).

That evening, deputies at hastily assembled wooden barricades were approached by another L. Hart & Son employee, O.M. Ennis, the advertising manager:

> "You'd better lay down your guns when we move in. You know what's good for you. We don't want any of you fellows hurt" (p. 202).

As the day progressed, San Jose radio station KQW peppered the airwaves with bulletin after bulletin (p. 203):

> "THE CROWD IS GATHERING! LYNCHING!

TONIGHT IN ST. JAMES PARK!"

Swift Justice captured the lethal delirium:

> "Other [radio] stations took up the cry, and late in the day traffic thickened on all highways as people piled into their cars and headed for the jail. From San Francisco and Oakland they came; from Gilroy and Morgan Hill and Salinas, from Santa Cruz on the coast" (p. 203).

> "They [lynchers] parked on First Street and went from one jammed tavern to another…drinking as they went. Blown-up photos of Brooke Hart's crab-eaten body were already being passed around the bars, . . ." (p. 203)

Ray Blackmore, later San Jose's police chief, was one of two young patrolmen who volunteered to help guard the jail the night of the lynching after San Jose Police Chief Black had ordered all San Jose Police officers to leave the jail. Sheriff Emig set Blackmore and another young patrolman in his office in the court house next to the jail where they had a clear view of the jail courtyard. Blackmore recounted his thoughts in *Swift Justice*:

> "The barricades were much too close to the jail door. Behind them was a driveway now jam-packed with probably five hundred people who should have been restrained far back, away out on the street. Still others were filling the park across the street. Altogether, the crowd was now approaching 2,000 " (p. 205).

Blackmore had dinner with Emig where he urged him to stand up to the mob:

> "What I said didn't sway him, because he was told what to do" (p. 205).

Irate San Jose mob dragging out Thomas Thurmond, after storming jail– *Courtesy of the Bancroft Library, University of California, Berkeley*

Blackmore called it an "execution" (p. 289).

All the pieces fell into place:

> "About six o'clock Santa Clara County Coroner Amos Williams received an ominous telephone message: 'Have a hearse in St. James Park at eleven o'clock tonight to pick up Holmes and Thurmond'" (p. 208).

Just before nine o'clock, the mob gathered at the wooden barricades was pushed from behind and the barriers splintered:

> "Ten or fifteen officers behind the barricades locked arms. For a few seconds, it seemed that the line would hold" (p. 209).

> "The noise of the tear gas bounced off the walls of the jail and the courthouse. The throng, thus challenged, was transformed" (p. 210).

St. James Park continued to fill as more and more people rushed to join the mob:

> "Hundreds of autos loaded with the concerned and the serious, responding to KQW's incessant stream of inflammatory bulletins, converged there and disgorged their passengers. How many? Most newspapers would use crowd figures of 5,000 to 15,000" (p. 214).

Governor Rolph kept abreast of the progress of the lynching:

> "All day in...Sacramento, Sunny Jim Rolph had been keeping track of the San Jose disorder with regular telephone reports from. . . Highway Patrol Chief Raymond E. Cato" (p. 215).

Two hours prior to the lynching, Rolph cancelled attendance at a western governors' meeting in Boise, Idaho.

The cancellation prevented his arch-rival, the lieutenant governor, from being granted the constitutional authority to call out the National Guard once Rolph had left the state.

In the sting of tear gas in the jail courtyard, a group of young men who manned an iron pipe finally felt the door to the jail break open.

On the third floor, Emig entered Thurmond's cell:

> "Sheriff, Thurmond whimpered, 'are they going to take me out and hang me?' "
>
> "Harold, it looks like we can't hold out. I'm afraid you may not have long to live. I'm going to ask you a question, and I want you to tell me the truth. Was anybody else in this thing with you and Holmes? Thurmond raised his hand and, with tears streaming from his eyes said:"
>
> "Before God, Sheriff, Holmes and I were alone on this job" (p. 223).

Thurmond's jail cell admission to Sheriff Emig was not the only lily gilded with guilt. The other was reported when mob members stormed into Holmes's cell:

> "Got anything to say you son of a bitch? One of the lynchers jumped the kidnapper, knocking him to the floor, out cold. They picked him up and slapped him back into consciousness. Who was in this thing with you, they demanded… .
>
> "[Holmes] Nobody but Thurmond." (p. 225).

Holmes, under ferocious attack from scores bloodthirsty mob members packed into his tiny cell, would have had to call a time-out in his desperate fight to survive just to state unequivocally that he and Thurmond were the only ones involved in the kidnap and murder of Brooke Hart.

Thurmond's laconic response had to be uttered during or immediately prior to his pitiable attempt to escape the mob as he suspended himself from an iron grate on the ceiling above a tiny toilet stall in his cell:

> "He was plumb crazy, trying to climb the walls like a monkey. He was squealing and leaping about…." (p. 225).

Both Holmes and Thurmond were taken into St. James Park. Holmes was dragged by a rope around his neck; Thurmond had been beaten unconscious.

> "They carried him [Thurmond], straightaway to a mulberry tree, across from the Elks Club and the Trinity Episcopal Church. Flashlights, arc lights, and spotlights from cars illuminated the grisly scene" (p. 230).

Thomas Thurmond strung to a tree in St. James Park across from San Jose jail– *Courtesy of the Bancroft Library, University of California, Berkeley*

The lynchers found an elm tree near the statue of President McKinley, where Holmes was raised to allow him to see the hanging body of Thurmond, lowered, then raised again.

> "Youths swigging bootleg booze…attacked Holmes with clubs and their fists, fingernails, and feet with no let up. Women lit matches and pressed them against his flesh. Younger thrill seekers broke into football chants: We want a touchdown! Block that kick! Hold that line!" (p. 233).

Holmes was lowered by the neck, then raised a third and final time:

> "The men on the rope gave a mighty yank. Scores of hands pulled slowly, deliberately until Holmes's feet were fifteen feet off the ground. He kicked the air and made two final grabs at the rope above his head, endeavoring to climb it hand over hand. Frantically, he tried to slacken the noose and jerk it free from his neck. The mob lowered him, broke his arms, and hauled him up again. The time was 11:25. Now, the hangmen melted anonymously into the throng of onlookers, unchallenged by the law officers watching helplessly from across the street" (p. 233).

The next morning, an ebullient Governor Rolph met with reporters:

> "I don't think they'll arrest anyone for the lynchings. They made a good job of it. If anyone is arrested for the good job, I'll pardon them all" (p. 241).

Special Agent in Charge Vetterli sent a memo to J. Edgar Hoover that disclaimed FBI responsibility for the lynching. When Thurmond and Holmes had been in the San Francisco city jail, the agents had taken them out for interrogation. Hoover had learned of it, and hand wrote a memo that advised them to stop because "If they were lynched while in our custody, it would be terrible."[10]

The Santa Clara County grand jury convened two months following the lynching and issued the following resolution:

> "[T]he testimony to this grand jury to date is totally inadequate to justify the bringing of any indictment against any person or persons for participation in the lynching of John M. Holmes and Harold Thurmond, and we have therefore failed to bring an indictment against anyone" (p. 268).

---

[10] FBI File

The end of the rope for Jack Holmes following San Jose jail attack and lynching– *Courtesy of the Bancroft Library, University of California, Berkeley*

Part VI FBI Handwriting Analysis

Jack Holmes and Thomas Harold Thurmond both confessed that Holmes wrote the three ransom notes to Alex Hart. Holmes was supposed to have had written the initial note on a postcard the night of the kidnapping in his car and then ordered Thurmond to mail it from Sacramento. Subsequently, Holmes had provided two additional letters that Thurmond mailed from, respectively, San Francisco and San Jose.

The week after the lynching, printed replications of the ransom demands completed by both Thurmond and Holmes had been finally analyzed by the FBI. The stunning result was not released to the public until 1983 when the fifty year statute of limitations on the confidentiality of the file had run its course:

> "After comparing them with specimens of both kidnappers' handwriting and printing, . . . they concluded they were Thurmond's work, not Holmes's, notwithstanding the admissions of the men" (p. 284).

The result constitutes evidence that both Thurmond's and Holmes's confessions had been concocted by the interrogators and signed under duress.

Swift Justice imagined a vignette that depicted the literacy of Thurmond in the creation of the third and final ransom demand:

> "[Holmes] Let's write another note to convince him.

"Thurmond again produced a writing tablet."

"What do you want to say?"

"Harold, you can't spell your own name" (p. 109).

The detailed specification of currency denominations, and the language employed by the author of the ransom cards and letters factually challenge the FBI finding that the dim-witted high school drop-out Thurmond could have formulated them. The question remains whether he wrote them at the direction of someone other than Jack Holmes.

Part VII Thurmond and Holmes

Little is known about the reaction of either Thurmond or Holmes after they were arrested for the kidnapping and murder of Brooke Hart and why, if they were innocent, each signed a confession. One reason is that Sheriff Emig would not permit them to be interviewed by the press, and allowed them only limited time with their family members and their attorneys.

Clearly, Thurmond's diminished mental and emotional state that prepared him for life as "Someone who would happily stick his head in an oven if asked to," made him the pin cushion upon which anything, including kidnapping, murder, extortion, and armed rrobbery could be stuck.

Thurmond was arrested after his third ransom and final ransom call to Alex Hart

> "What's your name, mister? [Sheriff] Emig demanded.
>
> "Harold Thurmond. What's this all about, sheriff?"
>
> "Who were you talking to?"
>
> "My mother" (p. 77).

Subsequently, Thurmond spoke over the telephone to members of the Hart family who had taken the ransom calls, then was brought to Sheriff Emig's office in the courthouse next to the jail.

> "You know why we brought you in, Harold?" Emig

asked him."

"No, sheriff, I've never been in trouble in my life. This is horrible for me."

"Where do you have Brooke Hart hidden?"

"My God, Mr. Emig, I'm a good boy. I go to church every Sunday."

"Then why did you snatch Brooke?"

"I didn't, I tell you. We're all religious people. My brother Roy, he's a preacher. And my sister's a church organist" (p. 113).

Arrested shortly after 8:00 p.m., Thurmond was grilled until midnight by Sheriff Emig, Undersheriff Hamilton, three FBI agents, Police Chief Black, and Governor Rolph's political ally and next door neighbor, attorney Louis Oneal. Around midnight, everyone left but Special Agent in Charge Vetterli:

"Those people [Hart family], have been suffering for a week, God wants you to show mercy now and put a stop to that. Tell me, can you swear before Almighty God that you did not kill Brooke Hart?

"Brooke Hart is dead, he blubbered."

"What did you do with him?"

"We threw him off the San Mateo Bridge."

"Who's in this with you, Harold?"

"His name is Jack Holmes. He lives here in San Jose" (p. 118).

At 3:30 in the morning, Thurmond, surrounded by Sheriff Emig, deputies, and FBI agents, knocked on the door of room 91 in the California Hotel. He was in the wrong place at the wrong time:

> "Jack?"
>
> "Who is it?"
>
> "It's me, Harold."

Holmes opened the door in his night clothes:

> "Police officers! You're under arrest, Emig shouted."
>
> "What the hell! What am I under arrest for?"
>
> "Murder."
>
> "This is all bullshit. I'm an honest family man, and I have to be out first thing in the morning looking for a job. Dammit, Bill Emig, tell these other sons of bitches who I am!"
>
> "Yeah, I know him" (p. 121)

Emig and Holmes had been fellow lodge brothers in the Masons for seven years. Holmes was dressed and taken to the courthouse for interrogation.

> "Your partner has implicated you, Jack," one of the FBI men told him. "It will be better for you if you tell us the truth."
>
> "I don't understand any of this," Holmes responded. "It has nothing to do with me" (p. 122).

The next day, Emig secretly brought Thurmond and Holmes to San Francisco because of the lynch threats. Emig later approached Holmes alone in his cell:

> "Well, Jack, as a Mason and a lodge brother, I can tell you that it will be best if you sign a confession" (p. 131).

Late that Friday, Jack received a visit from his wife:

> "Why on Earth did you sign a confession, Jack?" Again and again during the past forty-eight hours she had tried to recall every detail of what they had done on the kidnapping night, and had convinced herself that they had been together the whole time."
>
> "Jack …related how Emig, 'As a lodge brother,' had counseled him to confess. Unless he did so, the sheriff was going to turn him over to the San Jose mob. In the end, he decided to go along, believing he could easily prove his innocence once he got into court" (p. 143).

Jack Holmes probably believed he was right, as an attorney his wife retained obtained statements from the Estensens that confirmed Holmes's theater attendance on the night of the kidnapping (p. 142).

Upon his return to San Jose, Jack Holmes was allowed to meet with his father, Maurice:

> "Are you guilty, Jack?'
>
> "Dad,…I swear to you I know nothing about this." Holmes told his father his only connection with Thurmond was in a business deal; he was trying to sell Harold the old car he had driven before buying the Chevy.
>
> "Thurmond was offering $150 and I wanted $200" (p. 199).

VIII Veracity of the Confessions

The "face value" analysis of the confessions, eyewitness accounts of the kidnap victim seen with five men one half hour after his disappearance, alibi witnesses of Jack Holmes, and the results of the FBI handwriting analysis, establishes conclusively that neither Thurmond nor Holmes kidnapped or murdered Brooke Hart.

Swift Justice both anticipated and strongly challenged, however, any doubts about the veracity of the confessions:

> "For today's discerning inquirer, it flies in the face of plausibility to dismiss the confessions as fabrications out of whole cloth. Thurmond's was witnessed by six officers from three law enforcement agencies….Conceivably (though no clear evidence suggests it) pressures of public opinion or politics might have influenced local officers to falsify or doctor the documents, but what would have induced three out-of-town FBI men to abet such perjury?" (p. 282).

At the time of the Hart kidnapping, what had become the FBI in 1935 was an entity within the Department of Justice. At the time, J. Edgar Hoover had vigorously pursued the publicity necessary to ensure the political basis for the creation of an autonomous federal agency.

Between 1932 and 1935, the nation was beset with violent waves of gangsterism. Kidnappings like that of the Lindbergh baby always generated national media coverage. The Brooke

Hart kidnapping was just one of many high profile crimes from which the FBI obtained publicity.

The disavowal in *Swift Justice* about the complicity of the FBI in the creation or coercion of Thurmond's and Holmes's confessions didn't appropriately take into account its need to generate a solution of a crime for which Hoover would obtain public credit in the furtherance of his bureaucratic objective.

Special Agent in Charge Reed Vetterli's denigration of the only verified eyewitness accounts of the kidnapping, sanitization of the only eyewitness accounts from the summary report on the kidnapping, and complicity with the vigilantes in the lynching, strongly evidence that the FBI did "abet perjury" in the creation of Thurmond and Holmes's confessions.

J. Edgar Hoover's handwritten memo to the San Jose field agents about the possibility of a lynching evidenced worry solely over how the bureau would be affected, rather than about the mob murder of two possibly innocent men who had not even been arraigned for the crimes of which they were accused.

Part IX Middle-Class Mob

What allowed a middle-class population who lived in one of the most beautiful and safest valleys in the nation to abandon their law-abiding, God-fearing, conservative ways to participate in a mob assault on lawful authority?

It was not only the scores upon scores of men who spent hours in speakeasies acquiring liquid courage who made up the mob; entire families crowded into the park, grandparents and parents, aunts and uncles, boys and girls, and even infants in arms.

Once Thurmond and Holmes were dead, children were held up over the heads of the mob to see them hanging.

Law enforcement personnel, as prurient as everyone else, left the jail and the courthouse to witness both the lynchings and the mob celebration. The dead men, clothing stripped from their bodies, were disfigured by both men and women after their deaths. Once they were taken down, souvenir hunters fought over the ropes, and tore the bark off and ripped branches from the two trees.

Swift Justice recounted how one man got to the park in time for the lynchings:

> "They're getting ready to hang the sons of bitches. Come down and watch. Bring your wife."
>
> "Impossible, they couldn't leave their small daughter."

> "It's all arranged, I just talked to my wife. She's on the way to your house . . . ." (p. 219)

Of the 5,000 to 15,000 people who showed up, virtually no one, although more than one person may have felt compelled to do something, made any sustained attempt to stop the lynching. What permitted otherwise decent, honorable people to cheerlead the horrific murder of two men many knew and even grew up with?

Certainly the existence of the "committee of justice" composed of the most respected civic and business leaders in San Jose intimidated people from taking forceful action to stop the lynching. Another powerful restraint was the hold that political brokers had over the San Jose police chief who had been appointed by the San Jose City Council, and Sheriff Emig who had been elected with establishment money and political machinery linked to the California governor.

When all the civic, business, criminal justice, and moral leaders in a community possess identical contempt for the rule of law, how could the ordinary law-abiding citizen possibly stop such a juggernaut?

The governor of California, the highest elected constitutional official in the state, had not only refused to call out the troops, but promised to pardon anyone convicted of the lynching. Governor Rolph had provided a free pass for anyone who desired to commit a public murder, or just witness it to brag about it the rest of their lives. Literally thousands of Californians took him at his word, and Rolph was not proven wrong.

Thus was vaporized the everyday citizen's instinctual reluctance to participate in anarchy. Also gone was any semblance of individual responsibility; a mob did it.

Another important force that drove the lynching was the indictment of Thurmond and Holmes by the U.S. attorney. They weren't charged with the kidnapping and murder they deserved, only for mail fraud. When the U.S. marshals tried to take them into custody in San Francisco, the prisoners had to be rushed back to San Jose. Still not arraigned in Santa Clara County, Thurmond and Holmes remained legally vulnerable to the enforcement of the federal grand jury indictment.

In 1933, like today, much of the populace was highly suspicious and resentful of the enigmatic machinations of the criminal justice system.

An innocent young man with a promising life cruelly and dispassionately murdered, and the proven culprits are charged with the use of a mail box. Only a complaint of kidnapping had been issued against Thurmond and Holmes in Santa Clara County, and since there was no indictment or arraignment for murder, they could ultimately go free after being tried and sentenced for mail fraud in a federal court.

People were also exercised at the thought that Thurmond and Holmes might escape punishment that fit the crime because of an authority over which they held no political sway.

Certainly another prominent factor in the lynchings was the emotional atmospherics in play at the time. Did San Jose's inferiority complex described in *Swift Justice* contribute to the lynching?

Maybe San Jose wanted the "country cousin" chip knocked off its shoulders permanently.

Part X Conclusion

Whether the confessions of Thurmond and Holmes are taken at "face value" as in *Swift Justice,* or examined on the basis of objective facts, neither man is guilty:

- A woman and her daughter had witnessed five men with kidnap victim Brooke Hart near his car one half hour following his disappearance. Their eyewitness accounts had been verified by both Sheriff Emig and the FBI.

- Between 5:00 and 6:00 p.m. on the night of the kidnapping, Jack Holmes visited friends on the southern city limits of San Jose. He had departed near 6:00 p.m., and the distance to the L. Hart & Son store was such that the drive on surface streets would have let him arrive at L. Hart & Son after Brooke had been kidnapped.

- Holmes's wife, mother, and father stated he was home with them at 7:00 p.m. the night of the kidnapping.

- Gertrude Estensen stated that Holmes and his wife arrived at her home between 7:30 and 7:45 p.m. the night of the kidnapping.

- Thurmond claimed that Holmes's car was used in the kidnapping and murder, but during that time period, Holmes had his car with him at Ruth Gum's home, his home, or at the Estensen's home.

- The only eyewitnesses identified the kidnappers' car as being a large sedan. This matched the description of the car parked in the alley adjacent to the Hart store on ten consecutive days before the kidnapping, but not afterwards. Holmes's car was a two-door Chevrolet.

- Both Holmes's and Thurmond's confessions stated that Holmes composed and physically wrote three ransom notes. The FBI handwriting analysis determined that the notes were written by Thurmond. No fingerprints were found on any of the ransom notes or envelopes. Thurmond's arrested intellectual and emotional state evidences compelling doubt that he could have authored the ransom demands.

- The autopsy of the body revealed injuries to the skull that were due to the butt of a revolver, not from two blows to the head from a concrete block like Thurmond had confessed, or the result of the skull striking the pavement as Holmes confessed.

- Holmes and Thurmond both confessed that they had used a gun to kidnap and murder Brooke Hart, but no gun was ever found. The two wood gatherers had reported a cry for help, but no gunshots. No bullets were found in the body of Brooke Hart.

- Thurmond confessed that he had carried out his part of the kidnapping in his father's borrowed car. No confirmation of his use of this car appears in any available documentation about the Hart kidnapping and murder.

- Thurmond confessed to having thrown Brooke Hart's wallet into the San Francisco Bay between 10:30 and 11:00 p.m. the night of the kidnapping when the guardrail was still underwater. Because the wallet was found on the tanker guardrail, it had to have landed during the time Thurmond had confessed he was back in San Jose.

- Thurmond, intellectually and emotionally arrested in childhood by a severe head injury, confessed that he had made ransom calls to Alex Hart and negotiated the ransom delivery. Thurmond was mentally and emotionally incapable of the negotiation interaction documented in the public record.

- Jack Holmes, whose father had performed custom tailor work for L. Hart & Son, would have had known that Alex Hart had never learned to drive and not order that he repeatedly do so in ransom calls and letters.

Taken together or separately, these facts evidence that the confessions of Thurmond and Holmes were products of both manipulation and coercion. As a screaming homicidal mob broke down the door of the county jail, the fact that it was reported that both Thurmond and Holmes laconically affirmed that they were the only ones involved in the kidnapping, not only gilds the lily, it shoves a finger into the eye of the credibility of the case made for their guilt.

Because all the actions of Thurmond and Holmes are integrally joined in each of their confessions, if it is established that one man did not kidnap and murder Brooke Hart, then the other man could not have done it either. This means that both confessions were fabricated, and that the real kidnappers and murderers of Brooke Hart went free.

The only public inquiry conducted into the death of Brooke Hart was held a few days after the lynching by Alameda County coroner Grant Miller. Witnesses described Brooke Hart's departure from the store parking lot, the abandoned Studebaker, calls for help from the San Mateo Bridge, and the identification of Thurmond as the buyer of concrete blocks. The witness who sold the wire couldn't identify Thurmond as the purchaser.

The discovery of concrete blocks, one allegedly with blond hair stuck to it; wire; and a hat with a BrookHart label were held out as evidence that corroborated the confessions of both Thurmond and Holmes.

Because the body was in such an advanced state of decomposition, it would have been impossible—given the technology and chemistry at the time—to ascertain the pathology of Broke's death. Despite this fact, coroner's jury returned a verdict as to both the cause of death of Brooke Hart, and the identification of the persons responsible for it:

> "We find that Brooke Hart died on November 9 from asphyxiation due to submersion after he was first assaulted and cast from the San Mateo Bridge by Thomas H. Thurmond and John (Jack) Holmes, and we accuse Thurmond and Holmes of murder" (p. 258).

The inquest did not include the verification of the identity of the corpse.

Whether part of a kidnapping or as the result of a lynching, there is no statute of limitations on murder.

Exhibits

One: Executive Summary

San Jose, California, Thursday, November 9, 1933

Shortly after 6:00 p.m., twenty-two-year-old Brooke Hart was last seen in his new Studebaker President convertible roadster at the exit from the L. Hart & Son parking lot. When he failed to pick up his father, Alex Hart caught a ride with a colleague to a Chamber of Commerce meeting.

At 6:30 p.m., Delphine and Isabelle Silveria on their farm near Milpitas, seven miles east of downtown San Jose, saw a large sedan with three men in it stop near their barn. Shortly thereafter, a convertible with a man on each running board roared up next to it. The thin, light-haired driver of the convertible was placed in the larger car. There was no phone at the farm.

Three hours later, a telephone call was received at the Hart mansion. The male caller told Aleese Hart, Brooke's sister, that Brooke had been kidnapped. An hour passed, then a second male caller addressed Brooke's other sister Miriam by name, and stated that Brooke would be returned for $40,000. Instructions would come by phone the following day.

About midnight, Santa Clara County Sheriff William Emig learned that an abandoned car had been seen at 7:00 p.m. on Evans Road in Milpitas. It was Brooke Hart's Studebaker President convertible roadster. It was found a mile and a half north of the farm where eyewitnesses had seen the young man with five men.

Friday morning, a deckhand on an oil tanker in San Francisco found Brooke Hart's wallet on a guardrail. The previous night, the tanker had fueled a cruise ship. The fueling had commenced at midnight, and the weight of the fuel had kept the guardrail below the waterline until the middle of the early morning. The wallet was damp, not soaked, and investigators believed that it had been tossed directly onto the guardrail.

An L. Hart & Son employee reported that a 1931 Buick with two men in it had been seen in the alley adjacent to the store at 5:45 p.m. over the previous ten days. The description matched the car seen by Delphine and Isabelle Silveria.

The kidnappers did not contact Alex Hart until the following Monday, November 13th, when a ransom note, postmarked in Sacramento, was found in the L. Hart & Son mail.

Investigators believed that the kidnappers were amateurs because they threw Brooke's wallet away. This opinion was underscored by the absurd demand in the ransom note that a radio be installed in Brooke's Studebaker (it already had a radio), because ransom instructions would be broadcast over a radio station.

On Tuesday, November 14th, a second ransom note, this time postmarked in San Francisco, ordered Alex Hart to place $40,000 in the Studebaker and be ready to deliver it. Sixty-four-year-old Alex Hart had never learned to drive.

On Wednesday, a third ransom note postmarked in San Jose ordered Alex Hart to drive to Los Angeles with the $40,000 at ten miles per hour. Alex Hart placed a sign in the window of his store that stated he did not drive. At 8:00

o'clock that night, a ransom call was traced to a pay phone 150 feet from San Jose Police headquarters.

As twenty-eight-year-old local resident Thomas Harold Thurmond turned away from a pay phone in a parking garage, he was arrested by Sheriff Emig. At 3:00 o'clock the next morning, Thurmond confessed to the kidnap and murder of Brooke Hart on the San Mateo Bridge with a local man, Jack Holmes. The husband and father of two young children, recently unemployed and separated from his wife, Holmes was arrested in a hotel room at 3:30 a.m.

Word of Brooke's horrific death at the hands of two home town men intent to make a fast buck got out quickly. Because of immediate lynch threats, Sheriff Emig took the two men to the Potrero Hill police station in San Francisco.

The revulsion, then rage over the atrocities described in separate confessions signed by Thurmond and Holmes rocked the citizens of San Jose to their core.

Principal Discrepancies in the Confessions

Eyewitness Accounts

Brooke Hart's Studebaker was seen abandoned at 7:00 p.m. the night of the kidnapping, but at 6:30 p.m., two witnesses had seen the Studebaker, and a man who turned out to be Brooke Hart, being placed in a large sedan with five men two miles south from where the Studebaker was found. Jack Holmes drove a two-door Chevrolet.

Brooke Hart's Wallet

Thurmond confessed that he had thrown Brooke Hart's wallet into the San Francisco Bay between 10:30 and 11:00 p.m. and was back in San Jose by midnight. The guardrail of the oil tanker where the "damp but not soaked" wallet was found was underwater at midnight.

Holmes's Alibi

Both Thurmond and Holmes had confessed that they arrived in San Jose at 8:00 p.m. after the murder of Brooke Hart. A woman and her husband in San Jose stated that Holmes and his wife arrived at their home between 7:30 and 7:45 p.m. the same night prior to the four of them attending the movies.

Mastermind and Foil

Swift Justice author Harry Farrell portrayed Holmes as the kidnap mastermind, and Thurmond, whose intellectual and emotional growth had been arrested in childhood as the result of a severe head injury, as his foil.

Jack Holmes was the lamest criminal mastermind in recorded history:

- He kidnapped Brooke Hart near one of the busiest intersections in San Jose where numerous people could have easily recognized him, drove Hart in his own car bearing his license plates, and murdered him on a private toll bridge.
- He chose a hesitant, brain-damaged twenty-eight-year-old high school drop-out without a car that lived at home with his parents to negotiate the ransom with Alex Hart.
- He ordered Thurmond to borrow his father's car to mail ransom demands from different cities.

- He ordered Thurmond to throw Brooke Hart's wallet into the San Francisco Bay and not to remove identifying information.
- He ordered Thurmond to make a ransom call from a pay phone in a garage 150 feet from the San Jose Police headquarters.

Motivation

Swift Justice asserted it was the unrequited love for two materialistic women that made Thurmond and Holmes kidnap and murder Brooke Hart.

Two years prior to the kidnapping, Thurmond said he was engaged, but the woman had broken up with him because of his chronic poverty. On the day of the kidnapping, Thurmond had caught a glimpse of her and had "fallen to pieces," so in reaction, that night he kidnapped and murdered Brooke Hart.

Holmes, married eight years with two children, three days before he was arrested, split up with his wife over his alleged love for another married woman. *Swift Justice* insinuated how this love made him kidnap and murder Brooke Hart:

> "Slowly a plan for self-enrichment began to germinate in Holmes's febrile, criminally attuned, sexually haunted mind" (p. 90).

Ipso facto, love made Holmes and Thurmond kindred kidnappers, murderers and extortionists. In the court of public opinion, their angst over women was a perfectly sane reason for their utterly insane kidnapping of the scion of one of San Jose's most prominent families on a main street of the town where they had spent their entire lives.

Means

On the night of the kidnapping, Jack Holmes was gainfully employed and lived with his wife, two young children, and his mother-in-law. Holmes had nowhere to keep a victim, and no one to watch over a victim (Thurmond lived with his parents).

Thurmond didn't own a car, so each time Holmes ordered him to carry out a kidnapping task, he had to borrow his father's car.

Thurmond, described by his family and acquaintances as dull-witted, with the mentality of an "eight-year-old," was supposed to have carried out highly stressful, repeated ransom negotiations with a skeptical, highly intelligent, and experienced businessman, Alex Hart.

Indictment by Federal Grand Jury

November 22rd, four days prior to the lynching, a United States federal grand jury indicted Thurmond and Holmes for mail fraud. U.S. marshals attempted to take Thurmond and Holmes into custody at the San Francisco city jail, but the San Francisco police did not release them. Sheriff Emig quickly returned Thurmond and Holmes to San Jose.

Sheriff's Complaint

On the Friday before the lynching, Sheriff Emig signed a complaint that charged Thurmond and Holmes with the kidnapping, but not the murder of Brooke Hart. Thurmond and Holmes were never indicted or arraigned for either kidnapping or murder.

Governor's Promises

Jack Holmes's attorney requested the California governor, in the event of an attempted lynching, to call out the National Guard. Governor James "Sunny Jim" Rolph retorted:

> "If they lynch those fellows, I'll pardon the lynchers" (p. 193).

Rolph later told shocked reporters that he wouldn't send out the National Guard in San Jose to protect Thurmond and Holmes.

Two hours prior to the lynching, Rolph cancelled an out-of-state trip to a western governors' conference to prevent the lieutenant governor from calling out the troops in his absence.

The Body in the Bay

Early Sunday morning, four days before Thanksgiving, two duck hunters south of the San Mateo Bridge in a rowboat bumped into a terribly decomposed body. Sheriff Emig, L. Hart & Son employees, and a San Jose dentist later determined that the corpse was Brooke Hart.

The Lynching

Incessantly, throughout that Sunday when the body was found in the bay, radio stations broadcast bulletin after bulletin that a lynching would take place in San Jose that night.

Sheriff Emig prohibited firearms from being used against the lynchers. Sheriff's deputies, two San Jose policemen, and highway patrolmen were on duty, but as the mob swelled by thousands, they were characterized in *Swift Justice* as playing craps or pinochle.

Gas bombs spiked the rage of the mob. After a number of tries against the door to the jail with an iron pipe, mob members knocked it down and took Thurmond and Holmes from their cells.

Thurmond and Holmes were hanged from different trees.

Aftermath

The week after the lynching, the FBI completed the handwriting analysis of the ransom notes:

"They were Thurmond's work, not Holmes's . . ."[11]

Both Holmes and Thurmond had confessed that Holmes wrote the ransom demands.

The result of the FBI handwriting analysis was not made public for fifty years.

Following the arrest of Thurmond and Holmes, the Hart family had continued to receive written ransom demands and calls from different people who claimed Brooke was alive. The FBI, which had called its agents back to San Francisco after the arrests, had reopened its inquiry in San Jose.

Subsequent to the lynching, no additional efforts were undertaken to find the kidnappers and murderers of Brooke Hart.

---

[11] FBI File

Jack Holmes's parents sued Governor Rolph, but the suit was dropped when he died of a heart attack in the spring of 1934.

While hospitalized, Rolph fired a pistol loaded with blanks to summon hospital staff.

Two: The "Real" Kidnappers

Between 1932 and 1935, primarily in the Mid-west, the United States was besieged by what were characterized as "public enemies."

Pretty Boy Floyd, Alvin Karpis, John Dillinger, Machine Gun Kelly, and the like generated bold headlines throughout the country with brazen robberies, kidnappings, and wild shoot-outs with both local law enforcement, and agents of what would subsequently become the FBI.

They wielded Thompson sub-machine guns and drove powerful cars that quickly outdistanced cheaper law enforcement vehicles. These "public enemies" captured the imagination of the nation through their armed exploits, and often miraculous escapes from police traps and ambushes. Whenever it got too hot to operate in the Mid-west, they often traveled to live quietly on their illegal gains in California, Nevada, and Arizona.

When Brooke Hart was first kidnapped, information that "two hard-looking," "well-dressed," men had been seen outside the L. Hart & Son, and had tried to force Brooke off the road, prompted speculation the kidnappers were either Handsome Jack Klutas or Pretty Boy Floyd, gangsters who had been rumored to be in California.

The only eyewitness account that identified Brooke Hart with five men one half hour after his disappearance provides a plausible scenario for the kidnapping comedy of errors that affected the Hart family so horrifically, and cost Brooke Hart, Harold Thurmond, and Jack Holmes their lives.

After the five men abandoned Brooke Hart's highly visible Studebaker, they followed through with what the sole eyewitnesses overheard the night of the kidnapping.

Three of the kidnappers kept Brooke's wallet as evidence of his kidnapping, drove to San Francisco, and made the ransom calls. Two other kidnappers, Brooke Hart in hand, headed towards Sacramento, but not being locals, got on the San Mateo Bridge by mistake. One realized their vulnerability on a bridge with two exits, and ordered the driver to turn the car around and get off the bridge.

Brooke Hart saw his chance as the kidnappers turned around and jumped from the car. Too terrified to hesitate, Brooke leapt over the bridge railing into the darkness above the bay.

The wood gatherers heard cries for help but didn't find anyone.

Following the ransom calls, the other kidnappers, still in San Francisco, as stupid, selfish, and oafish as only criminals can be, celebrated their impending windfall in a number of speakeasies.

Sometime after three in the morning, they wandered drunkenly along the Embarcadero. Suddenly, one had the blurry epiphany that the police knew the ransom calls were made from San Francisco. If the police found Hart's wallet on them, they'd never get their share of the ransom money.

In intoxicated agreement with his prescient colleague, the kidnapper with Brooke Hart's wallet, without either hesitation or a look, tossed it off Pier 32. At that time of the early morning, the tanker guardrail was above the waterline. Miraculously, the wallet landed on it. They congratulated themselves over the knowledge that Brooke Hart was held at their hideaway.

The next day, one of the kidnappers that had been with Brooke spoke with the kidnapper who had thrown his wallet into the bay:

"Got the wallet?"

"Screw the wallet, you got Hart."

"Got the wallet, right?"

"Threw it into the bay."

"Threw it into the bay!"

"We don't need no wallet, you got Hart."

"Hart's gone."

"GONE!"

"Jumped off the bridge."

"What bridge?"

"Some bridge."

"He escaped?"

"YOU THREW HIS GODAMMED WALLET INTO THE BAY?"

"YOU LET HIM GET AWAY!"

They blamed each other for the wreckage of the biggest score of their lives, and split up.

Subsequently, both factions tried to bluff Alex Hart into a ransom payment. This could explain why ransom demands and calls were received from different people after the arrest of Thurmond and Holmes. None produced any physical evidence that they were Brooke Hart's kidnappers.

Three: Kidnapping, Murder, and Lynching Chronology

Mid-October 1933

Two men in a large sedan forced Brooke Hart's Studebaker against a curb; Hart sped away.

A man stated that he had sold a gun to Thurmond and that he appeared to have never handled a gun.

October 31

A concrete products salesman stated that he had sold three twenty-two pound concrete blocks to Thurmond.

October 31 – November 8

An L. Hart & Son employee stated that a 1931 Buick with two well-dressed men had been seen in an alley next to L. Hart & Son at 5:45 p.m. over ten-day period.

Wednesday, November 8

Holmes and Thurmond both confessed that they either met or didn't meet in Holmes's Chevrolet outside L. Hart & Son to plan Brooke Hart's kidnapping.

Thursday, November 9

5:00 p.m.

Holmes arrived at the home of Harvey and Ruth Gum on the southern city limits of San Jose.

Holmes confessed to being in his car outside the L. Hart & Son with Thurmond.

5:55 p.m.

Brooke got his Studebaker from the store parking lot to give his father a ride to a Chamber of Commerce meeting.

6:00 p.m.

An L. Hart & Son parking attendant last saw Brooke in his Studebaker at the exit.

Thurmond confessed to being in Jack Holmes's car outside L. Hart & Son.

Thurmond and Holmes both confessed that Holmes got in Brooke Hart's Studebaker at the L. Hart & Son Market Street exit, and at gunpoint, ordered him to drive to Evans Road in Milpitas.

Holmes left the home of Ruth Gum.

6:15 p.m.

Alex Hart (Brooke's father) sent an employee to find Brooke.

Alex Hart got another ride to the Chamber of Commerce meeting.

6:30 p.m.

Two witnesses saw Brooke Hart in his Studebaker near their barn in Milpitas. He was placed in a large sedan with five men.

7:00 p.m.

A housewife spotted a car abandoned outside her home a mile and a half north of the farm where witnesses saw Brooke Hart with five men.

Evelyn Holmes (Jack's wife), his mother, Hulda, and his father, Maurice, each stated that Jack Holmes was with them in San Jose.

Miriam Hart received a call from Charlie O' Brien (Brooke's friend) who said Brooke failed to appear at a class they were scheduled to attend.

Miriam called her father, who told her to call San Jose Police Chief Black.

Holmes and Thurmond both confessed that they had transferred Brooke Hart from his Studebaker to Holmes's Chevrolet at the point where the Studebaker was found abandoned.

Holmes and Thurmond both confessed that they drove Brooke Hart toward the San Mateo Bridge, turned around to get cigarettes left in Hart's Studebaker, and then drove thirty miles to the bridge.

Thurmond confessed that they drove Hart a half mile out from the eastern entrance to the San Mateo Bridge.

Holmes confessed that he drove three and one half miles to the drawbridge on the San Mateo Bridge.

Thurmond confessed that Holmes hit Hart twice on the head with a twenty-two pound concrete block.

Holmes confessed that he hit Brooke Hart with his fist.

Thurmond confessed that he bound Brooke Hart with wire.

Holmes confessed that Thurmond wired concrete blocks to Hart's feet.

Holmes and Thurmond both confessed that they threw Brooke Hart off the San Mateo Bridge.

Holmes confessed that Thurmond climbed over the railing, shot repeatedly at Brooke Hart in the water, climbed across the underside of the bridge and crawled up over the railing on the opposite side.

Thurmond did not confess that he had climbed under the bridge, or shot at Brooke Hart.

Holmes and Thurmond both confessed that Holmes turned the car around on the bridge.

Thurmond confessed that they stopped on the bridge, tossed a concrete block into the bay, and split the money in Brooke Hart's wallet.

Thurmond confessed that he kept Brooke Hart's wallet.

Holmes did not confess to anything about the wallet.

7:25 p.m.

Two men who gathered wood south of San Mateo Bridge heard cries for help.

Holmes and Thurmond both confessed that they drove back to San Jose some thirty-eight miles on the eastern side of San Francisco Bay.

7:30-7:45

Gertrude Estensen and husband stated that Jack Holmes and his wife arrived at their home for a movie date.

8:00 p.m.

Holmes and Thurmond both confessed that they had arrived at Fourth and Santa Clara Streets in downtown San Jose.

Holmes and Thurmond both confessed that Holmes wrote a ransom card, and gave it to Thurmond.

Alex Hart arrived home; Miriam drove him to police headquarters.

Chief Black asked the telephone company to trace calls to the Hart residence, and called Santa Clara County Sheriff William Emig, San Francisco police, and the FBI.

Thurmond confessed that he borrowed his father's car and drove to San Francisco.

8:20-8:30

Holmes and his wife and the Estensens left the Estensen's home for the Hester Theater in San Jose.

9:30 p.m.

Thurmond confessed that he tried and failed to make a ransom call to the Hart home from a speakeasy on Market Street in San Francisco.

Aleese Hart, Brooke's sister, stated that a man on phone told her that her brother had been kidnapped.

Alex Hart arrived home from San Jose Police headquarters.

10:30 p.m.

A man on the phone addressed Miriam Hart by name, and demanded $40,000 for Brooke. He would call next day with instructions.

Gertrude Estensen stated that she and her husband, and Jack Holmes and his wife went to a diner after the movie.

Thurmond confessed that he had made a ransom call from the Witcomb Hotel on Market Street in San Francisco to "some woman" at the Hart residence.

Thurmond confessed that he had thrown Brooke Hart's wallet into San Francisco Bay off Pier 32, walked back to his father's Pontiac, and drove to San Jose.

12:00 Midnight

The sheriff learned that Brooke's Studebaker was abandoned in Milpitas at 7:00 p.m.

An oil tanker commenced fueling the *Lurline* at Pier 32 in San Francisco.

Thurmond arrived back in San Jose.

Friday, November 10

FBI Special Agent in Charge Reed Vetterli arrived at the Hart mansion.

A phone trace revealed that the kidnap calls had been made from a speakeasy and a hotel on Market Street in San Francisco.

There was no sign of a struggle or fingerprints in Brooke's Studebaker.

A deckhand on an oil tanker in San Francisco found Brooke Hart's wallet on the guardrail.

A massive volunteer search for Brooke Hart commenced in remote areas of Santa Clara County.

Brooke had been reported seen in his Studebaker and at a speakeasy on the night of kidnapping.

No contact was made by the kidnappers with ransom instructions.

Thurmond confessed that he had met with Holmes; Holmes did not confess that he had met with Thurmond.

San Francisco police reported that Brooke Hart's wallet was damp which indicated that it had landed on the tanker guardrail, rather than floated onto it.

Thurmond confessed that he had borrowed his father's car, driven to Sacramento, and mailed ransom letter Holmes had provided him.

Saturday, November 11

A cruise ship fueled by an oil tanker in San Francisco was searched in Los Angeles, but there was no sign of Brooke or the kidnappers.

The volunteer search continued in Santa Clara County.

Thurmond had confessed that he met with Holmes; Holmes did not confess that he had met with Thurmond.

Brooke reported in Ross, Orland, and Los Angeles.

No contact from the kidnappers.

Sunday, November 12

The volunteer search continued in Santa Clara County.

No contact from the kidnappers.

Monday, November 13

The volunteer search continued in Santa Clara County.

The woman who had seen Brooke Hart with five men on the night of kidnapping contacted the sheriff.

A ransom letter postmarked from Sacramento was received at L. Hart & Son.

The FBI believed that the ransom letter was the work of a crank because of the order to put a radio in Brooke's Studebaker (which already had radio) so instructions could be broadcast over a radio station.

The sheriff and the FBI restaged the scene witnessed by the woman and her daughter at their farm to verify their recollections.

Vetterli sent a telegram to J. Edgar Hoover that reported that five men had kidnapped Brooke Hart. Vetterli also submitted a detailed account of the verification process used with the two eyewitnesses. The sheriff and the FBI kept the eyewitness accounts confidential.

No contact from the kidnappers.

Holmes confessed that he met with Thurmond and gave him a ransom letter to mail from Sacramento.

Thurmond confessed that he borrowed his father's car, drove to San Francisco, and mailed the second ransom letter.

Tuesday, November 14

A second ransom note postmarked in San Francisco on the previous night arrived in afternoon mail at L. Hart & Son. Alex Hart was ordered to place the money in the Studebaker, and drive to Los Angeles.

Holmes confessed that he met with Thurmond and gave him a ransom letter to mail in San Francisco.

Kidnappers, thought to be local men because they addressed Miriam Hart by name during the ransom call, didn't possess the common knowledge in San Jose that Alex Hart didn't drive.

Charlie O'Brien, Brooke's classmate who reported that he did not attend class the night of the kidnapping, was contacted on the phone by the kidnappers.

Alex Hart was ordered over the phone to take the night train to Los Angeles with the ransom. Hart did not go.

The FBI staked out the train station and apprehended a bank teller who was released upon identification by the sheriff.

A ransom call to Alex Hart was traced to a garage in downtown San Jose. Authorities arrived, but no one was on the phone.

Wednesday, November 15

A sign was placed in a L. Hart & Son window that stated that Alex Hart did not drive.

A third ransom demand postmarked in San Jose that day arrived with afternoon mail at L. Hart & Son that ordered Alex Hart to place the ransom in the Studebaker and drive at ten miles per hour towards Los Angeles.

A San Jose telephone operator reported that someone had tried to call the Hart home twice from pay phones ten blocks apart in downtown San Jose; neither call was completed.

Alex Hart spoke to a man over the phone who ordered him to drive to Los Angeles with the ransom, or have Charlie O'Brien do it. Hart argued with the man while the sheriff and the FBI raced to a pay phone 150 feet from San Jose police headquarters.

At 8:00 p.m., Thurmond was arrested at the pay phone in the parking garage.

Holmes confessed that he had parked across from garage where Thurmond made the ransom call. He failed to see scores of deputies, police officers, and FBI agents flood into the garage, and they failed to see him.

At 9:00 p.m. Holmes parked his car in the same garage where Thurmond was arrested. Holmes wore a blue suit with a panama hat, and was in a good mood.

Holmes confessed that he had gotten something to eat at a local tavern and went to bed. He never bothered to find out what happened to Thurmond.

Thursday, November 16

At 3:00 a.m., before he secured legal representation, Thurmond signed a confession in which he admitted to the kidnap and murder of Brooke Hart on the San Mateo Bridge with Jack Holmes.

At 3:30 a.m., Jack Holmes was arrested in a hotel room.

Because of the lynch threats, Thurmond and Holmes were brought to the Potrero Hill police station in San Francisco.

At 1:00 p.m., Holmes signed a confession that he had kidnapped and murdered Brooke Hart with Harold Thurmond on the San Mateo Bridge.

A search commenced for the body of Brooke Hart in the San Francisco Bay near the San Mateo Bridge.

Friday, November 17

The search of the bay continued.

Saturday, November 18

The search of the bay continued.

An Oakland Tribune article stated that the Hart family did not believe that Thurmond and Holmes murdered Brooke. No other paper carried the story.

Sunday, November 19

The search of the bay continued.

Monday, November 20

The search of the bay continued.

Tuesday, November 21

The search of the bay continued.

Wednesday, November 22

The search of the bay continued.

The U.S. attorney informed the press about the woman and her daughter who witnessed Brooke Hart with five men on the night of the kidnapping.

The Santa Clara County sheriff and agent Vetterli dismissed, as not credible, the sole eyewitness accounts of Brooke Hart on the night of the kidnapping.

A federal grand jury in San Francisco indicted Harold Thurmond and Jack Holmes for mail fraud.

U.S. marshals attempted to take Thurmond and Holmes into custody at the San Francisco city jail. They were rebuffed by the San Francisco police.

Santa Clara County Sheriff Emig took Thurmond and Holmes back to San Jose.

Thursday, November 23

Alienists examined Thurmond and Holmes in the Santa Clara County jail to preclude insanity pleas.

A mob remained outside the Santa Clara County jail day and night.

The search of the bay continued.

Friday, November 24

The search of the bay was called off.

Alex Hart posted a $500 reward for Brooke's body.

The Santa Clara County sheriff signed complaints against Holmes and Thurmond for the kidnapping, but not the murder of Brooke Hart.

Saturday, November 25

California Governor Rolph promised that he would pardon anyone convicted of lynching Thurmond and Holmes, and not call out the National Guard to protect them.

Sunday, November 26

Duck hunters found a terribly decomposed body in San Francisco Bay.

Sheriff Emig was advised that a body had been found, and word spread quickly throughout Santa Clara County.

Employees of L. Hart & Son and a San Jose dentist identified the body found in the bay as Brooke Hart.

Radio stations broadcast bulletin after bulletin about the lynching that was to occur in San Jose that night.

Highways and roads to San Jose were jammed with cars headed to the lynching.

At 9:00 p.m., the assault on the Santa Clara County jail began in earnest. Newspapers estimated that there were 5,000 to 15,000 men, women, and children in St. James Park.

At 9:00 p.m., Governor Rolph canceled a trip out of state to prevent the lieutenant governor from calling out the National Guard.

The Santa Clara County coroner was ordered to bring a hearse to St. James Park at 11:00 p.m. for the bodies of Thurmond and Holmes.

Thurmond and Holmes were hanged from separate trees.

Thurmond's and Holmes's bodies were cut down.

Monday, November 27

Governor Rolph reiterated his promise to pardon anyone convicted of the lynching of Thurmond and Holmes.

December 1933

The FBI analysis of the ransom letters determined that they were the product of Thurmond's handwriting. Both Thurmond and Holmes had confessed that Holmes had written them.

1934

The Santa Clara County grand jury found insufficient evidence to charge anyone with the lynching of Thurmond and Holmes.

Holmes's parents sued California Governor Rolph for the unlawful death of their son.

The FBI summary report on the kidnapping did not include the description of the only verified eyewitness accounts of Brooke Hart's kidnapping.

California Governor Rolph died of a heart attack; Holmes's parents dropped the lawsuit.

End Notes

From page 5

[i] Harry Farrell deserves a sincere debt of gratitude for memorializing a truly singular event in American political and criminal justice history that had been kept confidential by thousands of individuals for some nearly sixty years prior to the publication of *Swift Justice*. Mr. Farrell must be particularly commended for his candid and honorable disclosure of the facts he accepted at face value, and those did he did not. Mr. Farrell did the absolute best with what he had because of where he was born and lived, and that was no mean feat.

From page 10

[ii] In 1933, what was then called the Bureau of Investigation was part of the United States Department of Justice. In 1935, after a series of high-profile encounters with the likes of John Dillinger, Pretty Boy Floyd, and Alvin Karpis, this bureau was established as an independent agency in the executive branch called the Federal Bureau of Investigation (FBI). For purposes of clarity and simplicity, as was first done by Harry Farrell in *Swift Justice*, the Bureau is identified as the FBI.

Selected Bibliography

Books:

Farrell, Harry, *Swift Justice: Murder and Vengeance in a California Town,* St. Martin's Press, 1992.

Public Documents:

Brooke L. Hart Kidnapping File, Federal Bureau of Investigation.

Newspapers:

San Francisco Chronicle, November 10-29, 1933.
San Francisco Examiner, November 10-29, 1933.
San Jose Mercury Herald, November 10-29, 1933.
San Jose News, November 10-29, 1933.
Oakland Tribune, November 18, 1933.

Acknowledgments

Todd Stern, Weissman, Wolff, Bergman, Coleman, Grodin & Envall LLP

John Hammett, Proofreader/Editor

Public Relations by David Perry & Associates Inc.

Photographs Courtesy of the Bancroft Library, University of California, Berkeley

Design and Layout by Alfredo Casuso

John D. Murphy

John D. Murphy, among other roles, served as Senior Vice President for Institutional Affairs and Academic Vice President at the University of Phoenix, and as a member of the Executive Committee of the Apollo Group, a higher education holding company between 1977 and 1997.

Prior to his UOP experience, John taught at San Jose State University where he founded and directed Community of Communities, a mental health socialization and advocacy project with then former state mental hospital patients. Subsequently, he published and edited the Family Journal of Mental Health for families of the adult mentally ill.

Based on the only verified eyewitness account of the Brooke L. Hart kidnapping and his book and screenplay written (but both unpublished) on the Brooke L. Hart kidnapping in the 1980s, John, under the pseudonym 'Miles,' wrote a fictionalized screenplay, Valley of the Heart's Delight, which he produced as a feature film in 2006. Valley of the Heart's Delight won for Best Cinematography at the Boston International Film Festival, and a Silver Remi Award from WorldFest Houston in 2006.

Valley of the Heart's Delight
(www.valleyoftheheartsdelight.com), will be released theatrically in October 2007 by Intercontinental Drift. In 2007, 'Miles' completed his second feature film script, ICON, an action/thriller set in San Francisco.

www.ingramcontent.com/pod-product-compliance
Ingram Content Group UK Ltd.
Pitfield, Milton Keynes, MK11 3LW, UK
UKHW041944190726
13854UKWH00004B/1777

9 781430 326076